PIVOTAL
MOMENTS
IN HISTORY

THE
BLACK DEATH

DIANE ZAHLER

TWENTY-FIRST CENTURY BOOKS
MINNEAPOLIS

For Phil

Consultant: Joseph P. Byrne, Historian and Professor of Honors, Belmont University, Nashville

Acknowledgments:
I would like to thank the following people for their invaluable help: Debra Cardillo, for knowing all the right people; Peter Zahler, for knowing all about tarabagans; Stanley Zahler, for knowing all about bacteria; and Philip Sicker, for knowing everything else.

Primary source material in this text is printed over an antique-paper texture.

The image on the jacket and cover is a fourteenth-century fresco from Saint Sebastian's chapel in Lanslevillard, France, showing a physician lancing a plague-caused bubo.

Twenty-First Century Books
A division of Lerner Publishing Group, Inc.
241 First Avenue North
Minneapolis, MN 55401 U.S.A.

Website address: www.lernerbooks.com

Library of Congress Cataloging-in-Publication Data

Zahler, Diane.
        The Black Death / by Diane Zahler.
            p.   cm. — (Pivotal moments in history)
        Includes bibliographical references and index.
        ISBN 978–0–8225–9076–7 (lib. bdg. : alk. paper)
        1. Black Death—Europe—History. I. Title.
    RC178.A1Z34 2009
    614.5'732—dc22   2008026878

Manufactured in the United States of America
1 2 3 4 5 6 – BP – 14 13 12 11 10 09

CONTENTS

CHAPTER ONE

ON THE EDGE OF THE ABYSS

In the year of our Lord 1315, apart from the other hardships . . . hunger grew in the land.

—Johannes de Trokelowe, 1300s

Avian influenza, or bird flu, has been in the news a lot. Scientists fear that the virus that causes it may mutate and create a human pandemic—a worldwide epidemic. If that were to happen, health officials estimate that 2.5 percent of the world's population might die. That's two to three people out of every one hundred. Imagine how the world would change if that occurred. Society, economics, and even the way people practice religion would be profoundly affected.

Imagine that instead of 2.5 percent of the population dying, 30 to 60 percent died—thirty to sixty out of every hundred people. That's what happened in Europe between 1347 and 1352, the years of the first wave of the bubonic plague. Entire families, neighborhoods, and even towns succumbed to the disease in a matter of days. The effects of such wide-scale death and devastation were enormous. Manor houses, shops, and farms were emptied of people, so normal business fell apart and had to be restructured. Society had to rebuild. People had to reconsider the way they thought about life and death.

NORTHERN EUROPE IN THE FOURTEENTH CENTURY

When people think of Europe in the Middle Ages, or the Medieval Period (A.D. 500–1500), they often picture knights in gleaming armor, ladies in trailing velvet gowns, and minstrels singing love poetry in the marble halls of castles. This is largely because of romantic novels and Hollywood movies. The Middle Ages didn't really look much like that. The wealthiest nobles and kings lived in manors or castles, wore fine clothing, and dined well. But even they could not escape the dirt of daily life and the dangers that went with it.

In the 1300s, the century of the Black Death, the vast majority of Europeans were poor. In the north, in modern-day Britain, France, the Netherlands, Belgium, Germany, and Austria, 90 percent of the population lived in the countryside. Most lived in small villages in the shadow of a manor house. The lord of the manor was at the top of the local social order. Below him were the freemen—farmers or craftspeople

Serfs harvest grain under the direction of their lord's official in this English painting from around 1310.

who owned their own land. Craftspeople might include blacksmiths, carpenters, and millers. At the bottom of the social order were the landless serfs—farmers and craftspeople with few rights or possessions. The lord owned the land on which the serfs lived and worked, or he managed it for his own overlord. The serfs had to work for this lord several days each week to pay rent on land to farm for themselves.

Villagers lived in small houses, often built of wattle and daub. This is a woven frame of branches covered with clay mixed with straw and cow manure. The floor of the house was earth, sometimes spread with straw or rushes, a plant that grows in marshy areas. The roof was made of thatch (straw, grasses, or other plant material). If there was a window, it had no glass. It was open to the air in warm weather and shuttered in the cold. Goats, chickens, pigs, and sometimes cattle shared the space with the family for their protection at night and to add warmth in winter. The air indoors was smoky from the fire that constantly burned on the hearth.

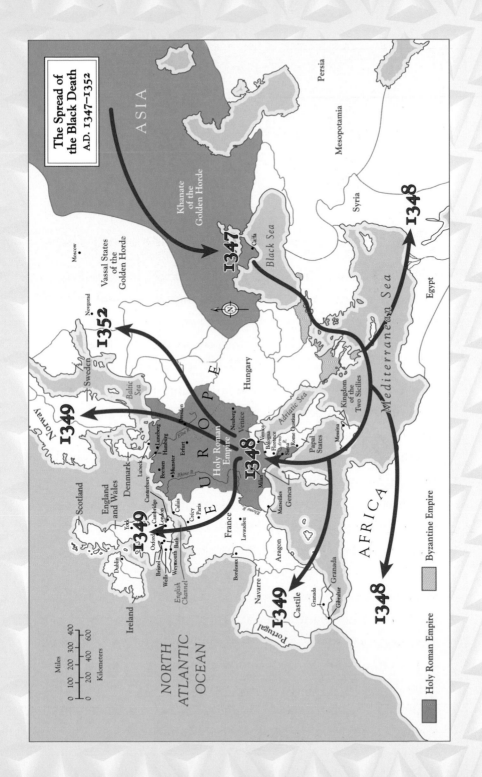

The Spread of
the Black Death
A.D. 1347–1352

ASIA

Persia

Mesopotamia

Khanate
of the
Golden Horde

Vassal States
of the Golden Horde

Moscow

1347

Caffa

Black Sea

Syria

1348

Egypt

Mediterranean Sea

Novgorod

1352

Sweden

Baltic Sea

Hungary

Adriatic Sea

Kingdom of the Two Sicilies

Papal States

Rome Ostia

Messina

AFRICA

1348

Norway

1349

Denmark

Lübeck

Hamburg

Bremen

Münster

Neuberg

Dresden

Erfurt

Elbe R.

Holy Roman Empire

E U R O P E

Rhine R.

Milan

Venice

Bologna

Florence

Arno R.

Siena

Genoa

Marseilles

Rhône R.

Scotland

England
and Wales

York

Canterbury

Cambridge

London

Oxford

Bristol Bath

Weymouth Wells

Crécy Paris

Calais

France

Lavaudieu

Bordeaux

Navarre

Aragon

Castile

Portugal

Granada

Gibraltar

1349

Ireland

Dublin

English Channel

NORTH
ATLANTIC
OCEAN

Miles
0 100 200 300 400
0 200 400 600
Kilometers

N

1348

Holy Roman Empire

Byzantine Empire

AT HOME WITH ANIMALS

Families in the country who slept with their animals had an average of 9.6 rats per household. Families who didn't share their homes with livestock averaged 8.2 rats.

In the fourteenth century, trade routes were opening because of changes in the medieval economy, increased exploration, and advances in shipbuilding. Nearby towns grew as trade centers. Merchants and tradespeople lived in these towns and depended on one another for basic services and supplies. Towns and cities had walls to enclose them and protect their inhabitants from bandits and invaders. Within the enclosure, houses were pressed closely together, often sharing walls. They blocked the sun from the narrow streets below. The streets were usually unpaved, and in rainy times, they became muddy and impassible.

Most cities in northern Europe at the time were quite small. London and Paris had well over fifty thousand inhabitants, but the population in other cities ranged from three to twenty thousand. As trade flourished, a small but wealthy middle class developed. A well-to-do tradesman might live in a four-story house with a business on the ground floor, making and selling anything from ale to shoes to barrels. Living quarters would be found on the upper floors. A wealthy family might have strong oak furniture; wear warm, well-made clothing; and spend money on spices for their food. Still, their houses were not clean.

LIFE IN ITALY AND THE SOUTH

Italy in the 1340s was not a unified country. The southern part of the peninsula was ruled by Charles II, a French prince, and the large island of Sicily was ruled by Frederick III, the Holy Roman Emperor. Farther north the territory was divided into independent city-states, including Venice, Milan, Genoa, and Florence.

Venice, in the east on the Adriatic Sea, and Genoa, in the west on the Mediterranean Sea, were the most powerful coastal cities. Both were ports and centers of trade. Inland, Florence had become the most influential city-state by the 1300s. Both Florence and Venice were centers of banking and places of great wealth. They were republics, governed by councils. They and Milan each boasted close to one hundred thousand inhabitants by the end of the thirteenth century. Other cities, such as Bologna and Verona, had populations of at least fifty thousand. Rome was a much smaller city at that time and was rife with crime. The rest of the peninsula was dotted with towns, villages, and farms that provided the food for the cities.

The Iberian Peninsula—modern-day Spain and Portugal—was divided into five kingdoms in the 1300s. These included the kingdoms of Castile, Aragon, Navarre, Portugal, and the kingdom of Granada ruled by people from northern Africa known as Moors. Conflict among and within the kingdoms raged almost continually. Until the mid-1200s, the Moors, whose religion—Islam—followed the teaching of the Quran and the Muslim prophet Muhammad, had held much of the peninsula. By the mid-thirteenth century, the king of Castile had pushed them to Granada, their only outpost left on the continent. Civil wars plagued Castile and Aragon, leaving the people and their governments weakened.

THE MEDIEVAL ECONOMY

In cities, towns, and villages of medieval Europe, most production and commerce was controlled by guilds—organizations of masters who hired and trained workers. Guilds appeared in Europe as early as the tenth century. By the 1300s, these organizations were strictly structured and regulated. The two major types of guilds were merchant and craft. In merchant guilds, guild members enforced contracts, sometimes by seizing goods belonging to a person who broke a contract. Guild members protected one another from overtaxing by foreign officials by threatening to boycott the lands of rulers whose tariffs (taxes) were too high, and they often were powerful enough to influence local government.

Craft guild members usually owned small businesses or workshops. Butchers, textile workers, bakers, carpenters, shoemakers, and clerks were some of the businesspeople likely to be members of a craft guild. Both types of guilds had a similar structure. At the top were the masters, men who owned their own shops or ships for trading. Below them were the journeymen, workers who received wages for working for a master or for short-term jobs with several different masters. At the bottom were the apprentices, usually young men or boys who worked for room and board and the chance to learn a trade from a master.

Merchants conduct their business in the streets of an Italian city.
Created in the city of Siena in the early 1300s, this painting celebrates
the blessings of peaceful government.

A cloth merchant displays his wares for a buyer. The image comes from a book of rules for the English Guild of Drapers (cloth sellers). It was created in the early 1300s.

Craft guilds were important in regulating both the workmanship of materials and the pay that members received. Many guilds required a stamp of the guild's approval on each item sold. Guilds regulated prices and closely guarded secrets of their trade. Guilds took care of their members. They paid for funerals of members who died and helped their widows and children, built chapels for worship, and provided care for the sick.

THE MEDIEVAL CHURCH

Europe was mostly Catholic in the Middle Ages. The head of the Catholic Church was the pope, who until the beginning of the fourteenth century lived in Rome. The pope was elected by a group of cardinals, clergymen who were usually bishops. The cardinals' other main responsibility was to advise the pope, and most popes came from this group. Below them in the hierarchy were bishops, priests, monks, and lay brothers. Geographically, areas were organized into parishes, each with its own priest. The parishes were grouped into dioceses, each led by a bishop.

Medieval life revolved around the seven sacraments of the church, the key ceremonial rites of Catholicism. In the sacrament of baptism, a child becomes a member of the church. Confirmation fully initiates worshippers into the church. In doing penance, worshippers confess sins they have committed to a priest. The priest sets a penance for the sinner, and when it is performed, the penitent is forgiven. In the sacrament of Holy Eucharist, a priest gives worshippers wine and wafers that they believe have become the blood and body of Christ. This nourishes the worshipper spiritually. Matrimony is the sacrament of marriage. In holy orders, believers take vows and become priests. The sacrament of last rites prepares a dying person's soul for heaven.

The Catholic Church controlled much of medieval life, from legal matters to scholarship to medicine. Few people besides monks and priests could read. Those who could read had been taught by monks in schools run by their monasteries. Monasteries also ran trade schools, where monks taught students such skills as embroidery and goldsmithing, so they could make the decorated articles for the church. Convents, which housed nuns, educated girls in the ways of the church and provided charity for the local community. The church also operated hospitals, and nuns and monks provided most of the care of patients. It also built and maintained many roads and bridges. Until around 1300, the Catholic Church was very nearly all-powerful.

In 1303, however, Philip IV of France decided that as king, he could levy a tax on the French clergy. Appalled at this, Pope Boniface VIII accused him of crimes against the church and summoned him to Rome. In response, King Philip declared the pope guilty of, among other things, sorcery (witchcraft) and heresy (denying church beliefs) and sent soldiers to arrest him. Boniface was quickly freed, but he was quite old at the time, and the shock to his papal dignity killed him.

The next pope to be elected was a Frenchman, Clement V, and he chose not to go to Rome. Instead, he decided to reside in the town of Avignon in the south of France. There he and the popes who followed him created a papacy that was known for its extravagant way of life. They built an enormous papal palace, filled with lavish furnishings and rich tapestries. Nunneries and monasteries sprang up around it. Clement VI, who was pope in the mid-fourteenth century, had more than one thousand ermine skins to wear, a staff of more than four hundred, and a zoo.

This 1305 portrait shows Pope Clement V about to go hunting with a hawk.

MEDIEVAL SIGHTS AND SMELLS

Both city and countryside, north and south, were filthy and smelled. In the country, there was the stink of livestock, animal waste, and unwashed humans. Though people did wash in the Middle Ages, only the wealthy could afford to heat enough water for a bath on a regular basis. Washing hands and faces was part of many people's daily ritual, but baths and clothes washing happened only rarely.

Other smells, both in city and country, included the tallow, or beef fat, from which most candles were made

This 1356 illustration from an Italian book of medicine shows a woman helping a sick man bathe. Some medieval doctors ordered patients to wash more frequently until they recovered.

and the fish oil used in lamps. In the city, the stench of animal waste from the dogs and pigs that roamed freely (and sometimes died) in the streets would be sickening. Added to this were industrial wastes from businesses such as tanning (turning animal skins into leather) and dyeing and the odor of human waste from cesspits and chamber pots.

All this waste made its way into the water table. Streams and rivers were heavily polluted. Even wells were likely to be contaminated. Only a few people at this time recognized that this filth posed a serious health hazard. King Edward III of England tried to address the problem, issuing a royal writ in 1305. He noted that

> brewers of ale . . . draw and collect water for brewing near sewers and in other unclean places, which are polluted and infected. Consequently, the ale produced from the same, which is sold to the masters and students and to others living there for their sustenance, is not as wholesome and as nourishing as it ought to be, causing them no slight harm and the evident detriment of their health. . . . We order you to have the brewers of the town draw and collect water for brewing ale in clean places, where the water is found to be fresh and pure, and not elsewhere.

But there was nowhere for the waste to go besides into the waterways. Sewer systems, in those towns and cities that had any, were only a series of gutters that emptied into local streams and rivers. These gutters emptied only

LOOK OUT BELOW!

In London in the fourteenth century, a city law stated that a person must call, "Look out below!" three times before pouring out the contents of a chamber pot onto the street below. Woe betide those who didn't have time to get out of the way!

when it rained. The rest of the time, the waste simply sat there, stinking.

These unsanitary conditions, both in the city and the country, attracted such pests as flies, lice, fleas, and rats. One fourteenth-century husband wrote to his wife about the problem.

> In summer take heed that there be no fleas in your chamber nor in your bed, which you may do in six ways, as I have heard tell. For I have heard from several persons that if the room be scattered with alder leaves the fleas will get caught therein. . . . Take a rough cloth and spread it about your room and over your bed and all the fleas who may hop onto it will be caught, so that you can carry them out with the cloth wheresoever you will.

LIVING AND DYING

Food in the Middle Ages was usually bland and unvaried. All over Europe, the diet was based on bread. Everyone, children as well as adults, drank ale, wine, and hard cider.

In the north, bread was supplemented by cheese, herring, cabbage, and peas. Meat was expensive so most people didn't eat it regularly. In France, people occasionally ate cooked fruit, and in Italy, pasta was often on both peasant and noble tables. This limited diet led to tooth decay, skin trouble, and frequent infections.

Diseases such as typhoid, dysentery, smallpox, and influenza struck frequently. Life expectancy was far shorter than it is in modern times. In fact, the average life expectancy at birth in 1300 was only about thirty-three years. This number is so shockingly low in part because infant and childhood mortality was so high. Babies were very likely to die at birth or shortly afterward. However, if a boy lived to the age of ten, he could expect to live about another thirty-two years, and if he made it to twenty, he could expect to survive to fifty-two. Females were more likely to die between the ages of fourteen and forty because childbirth was so dangerous. Before fourteen and after forty, though, a woman's life expectancy was greater than a man's.

Another factor that influenced health and shortened life span was war. The Hundred Years' War (1337–1453) was fought between England and France. It continued off and on for more than one hundred years, taking the lives of thousands of able-bodied young men and leading to the deaths of countless more civilians. Other conflicts flared up at intervals all over Europe. Many clashes included a siege, in which enemy forces surrounded a town or castle and starved it into submission. Soldiers' camps were filthy, and disease and death were common even when weapons were not drawn.

THE GREAT FAMINE

In the early 1300s, life grew even harder. All over Europe, the weather cooled, producing what later scientists called a little ice age. Winters were colder than before, and summers were cool and very wet. As a result, harvests were bad. The balance between population and food supply, which had been stable for decades, started to shift. Suddenly there was not enough food, and people across Europe began to starve.

During the years 1314 to 1317—known as the Great Famine—10 to 15 percent of the population of Europe starved to death. Johannes de Trokelowe, writing in the fourteenth century, described this time.

> The summer rains were so heavy that grain could not ripen. . . . The usual kinds of meat, suitable for eating, were too scarce; horse meat was precious; plump dogs were stolen. And, according to many reports, men and women in many places secretly ate their own children.

When the Great Famine ended, European society rebounded to some extent. The population grew again after 1317, but resources were still low. And the famine had weakened people in ways they could not imagine. Starvation, in the very young, interferes with the development of the immune system. As a result, those who had lived through the famine were less likely to be able to fight off disease. By the 1340s, the generation born thirty years earlier was less healthy and resistant to disease than their parents had been.

THE OPENING OF THE EAST

Western Europe, in the early 1300s, was opening up to other cultures. In the 1270s, an Italian merchant, Marco Polo, had traveled through central Asia to China, and fifty years later, there were Italian colonies in China. East-west trade routes carried goods from Asia and the Middle East to the markets of England, France, and Italy. One medieval writer, William FitzStephen, describes seeing these new items in the markets of London.

> Gold from Arabia, from Sabaea spice
> And incense, from the Scythians arms of steel
> Well-tempered; oil from the rich groves of palm
> That spring from the fat lands of Babylon;
> Fine gems from Nile, from China crimson silks;
> French wines, and sable, vair, and miniver [furs]
> From the far lands where Russ and Norsemen dwell.

Although these goods increased the demand for trade with the East, those "far lands" contained dangers of their own. In the early 1200s, a group called the Mongols—unified under their chief, Genghis Khan—had conquered most of northern China and central Asia. In 1235 they held a meeting of their leaders and decided to move westward. Their aim was not trade but conquest. And eventually they set their sights on the wealth of Caffa, an Italian trade colony on the shores of the Black Sea bordering modern-day Russia and Turkey. The Mongols, however, carried with them an invisible threat far greater than their weapons and their skill at warfare.

Marco Polo's caravan appears on a 1375 map of central Asia and China. The map comes from the Catalan Atlas, which was created in the Kingdom of Majorca (modern-day Spain).

THE STAGE IS SET

In 1347 western Europe teetered on the brink of disaster. Climate change three decades earlier had created famine, weakening the population. War and filthy living conditions bred vermin that carried diseases. The opening of trade routes brought not only new goods and new cultures but new dangers. Even the earth and skies themselves seemed to be preparing for catastrophe. Volcanic eruptions and earthquakes were reported in Italy, floods overran Germany and France, and a tidal wave hit Cyprus. It would take only the bite of a single flea to create that catastrophe.

CHAPTER TWO
FROM FLEA TO HUMAN

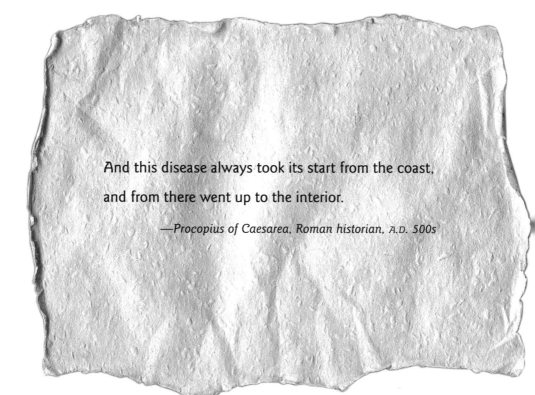

And this disease always took its start from the coast,

and from there went up to the interior.

—*Procopius of Caesarea, Roman historian*, A.D. 500s

All plague is caused by the bacterium *Yersinia pestis*. It was named after the Swiss microbiologist Alexandre Yersin, who, along with Japanese scientist Shibasaburo Kitasato, finally isolated the bacteria in 1894. The bacterium lives mostly in small mammals, such as rats, squirrels, marmots, and other rodents. In many of these populations, plague is enzootic. That means it is constantly present in the mammals but affects only a small number of animals at any one time. It

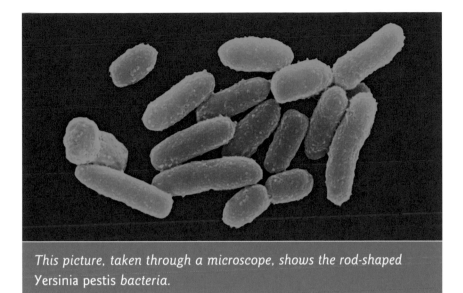

This picture, taken through a microscope, shows the rod-shaped Yersinia pestis *bacteria.*

may be because the bacterium has become weaker, or it may be that many of the rodents have become resistant to it. The animals that carry the bacterium may not get sick, but they still are able to transmit *Yersinia pestis* to the fleas that bite them and suck their blood.

One such flea, with the scientific name *Xenopsylla cheopis*, has a forestomach in which the plague bacteria multiply quickly. The bacteria grow to such huge numbers that the digestive tract of the flea becomes blocked, and the flea cannot get its food—the blood of its host. It gets very hungry, and when it bites its next victim, it transmits a flood of the bacteria that have built up inside it. Scientists estimate the flea will spit out between eleven thousand and twenty-four thousand bacteria into its host, more than enough to cause disease. The flea can live for up to six weeks with its blocked digestive tract. During that time, it will jump desperately from host to host, trying to feed and spreading its bacteria.

Xenopsylla cheopis *is also known as the Oriental rat flea.*

The flea X. *cheopis* originally lived on central Asian marmots, particularly a marmot called the tarabagan, which lives on the steppes (plains) of Mongolia. The plague has been enzootic in the tarabagan population for a long time. Occasionally, it becomes epizootic, which means it causes widespread disease among the marmots. This occurs either because the bacteria mutate and become stronger or because the marmot population is stressed in some way—by another disease or by hunger, for example. When that happens, the marmots die of plague, and their fleas must find new, living hosts.

Black rats can also act as the host for the X. *cheopis* flea. Black rats make their home among humans. If a rat is infected with *Yersinia pestis* and dies or if a rat's fleas have

INSECT ANTICS

A flea can jump as much as 6 inches (15 centimeters) horizontally and 4 inches (10 cm) vertically. This makes frequent movements from host to host fast and easy for the tiny insect.

Black rats can be found on every continent on Earth. They eat many different types of plants and insects. Rat populations increase around human settlements, where they feed on fruit and grain crops.

their digestive systems blocked by plague bacteria, these fleas will leap off and try to find another host—often a human one, if no rats are available. All that is needed for plague to move from tarabagan to human is contact between the fleas of tarabagans and rats. Since black rats are abundant on ships at sea, they can carry the fleas and their bacteria from seaport to seaport.

Plague can be passed to a human through the bite of a flea. The bacteria can also enter through the skin. If the flea defecates on a person's skin and the person scratches enough to break the skin, the bacteria can enter through the scratch. When the plague is contracted in these ways, it is called bubonic. The bubonic plague bacteria incubate from one to six days as the number of bacteria grows. After one to six days, as the number of plague bacteria increases, victims will feel a headache, weakness, chills, and fever. They may develop a white coating on the tongue and a rapid pulse. Inside the body, the bacteria create a poison that kills tissue cells. The bacteria move throughout the body in the bloodstream, building up to such numbers that they clog small blood vessels and the vessels burst. The bacteria then move to the lymph nodes, which would ordinarily produce antibodies to kill the bacteria. By then, though, the bacteria's numbers are so huge that the body's defenses are overwhelmed. The lymph nodes containing the bacteria enlarge to form swellings called buboes. If the fleabite is on the legs, buboes will probably develop in the groin. (The word *bubonic* comes from the Greek word *boubon*, which means "groin.") If the bite occurs higher on the body, buboes might appear in the lymph nodes of the neck or the armpits.

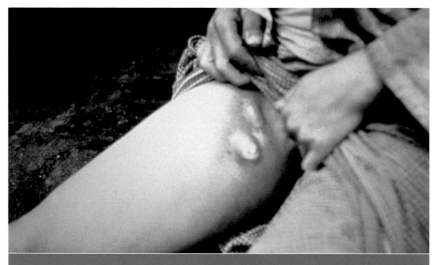

This 1993 photo shows buboes on a person's upper thigh. They were caused by the bubonic plague bacteria.

They can grow as large as an apple and are very painful because they press on nerves. Left untended, they may eventually burst. Small red or black spots caused by leaking blood vessels may also appear on the skin.

The infected person will suffer convulsions and dizziness, may vomit blood, and will feel intense pain in the arms and legs. Death is often rapid, within a matter of days. Scientists estimate that at least 60 and as many as 90 percent of those infected with bubonic plague will die if untreated. Some of those who survive might do so because of a genetic mutation that creates immunity. Others who live untreated are likely to have been better fed and in better general health than those who died.

The plague has two other forms, both faster and even more often fatal than the bubonic form. In septicemic plague, which is probably also transmitted by a fleabite, there is almost no incubation period. The bacteria infect the bloodstream, the circulatory system collapses, and the patient bleeds internally. Death occurs within twenty-four to thirty-six hours, usually so quickly that the painful buboes do not have time to form.

In pneumonic plague, bacteria infect the lungs directly, causing congestion, fluid buildup, and a bloody cough. Victims develop a high fever and fast pulse rate. Infected persons drown in their own fluids. It takes one to three days after infection for pneumonic plague to show symptoms, but as soon as visible signs are present, death will occur within forty-eight hours. This kind of plague can be spread by speaking, coughing, or sneezing, and so it is more highly contagious than the other forms, which require the bite of an infected flea.

In the Bible, God sends a plague of boils, or unhealable swellings, to punish an Egyptian king. The Swiss painter of this 1411 Bible page used people with buboes to represent this plague.

THE PLAGUE IN EARLY HISTORY

It is possible that plague was present in biblical times. In the Old Testament, the first Book of Samuel mentions a plague suffered by the Philistines that had as one of its symptoms boils or tumors, which may have been buboes. Indications of plague appeared in ancient Egypt too. An archaeologist recently found an Egyptian medical text called the Ebers Papyrus, dating back to 1500 B.C. It describes a disease with symptoms including buboes, which modern scientists take to be plague. The ancient Greeks described occasional small outbreaks of what sounds like plague in North Africa and the Middle East. It wasn't until 541, however, that the first documented plague pandemic broke out.

At that time, the Byzantine Empire controlled much of the Mediterranean. Ruled by Justinian I, the empire included parts of northern Africa, Greece, Italy, Spain, and much of the Middle East. Constantinople, the present-day port city of Istanbul in Turkey, was its capital. As many as half a million people lived in the city.

To feed such a large population, Justinian imported grain from Egypt and elsewhere in Africa. Along with the grain came the rats that ate it. Historians believe that those black rats and their fleas, infected with plague, originated either in Egypt or in Ethiopia. The historian Procopius wrote about the start of the disease:

A portrait of Emperor Justinian I from around 550

It started from the Aegyptians [Egyptians] who dwell in Pelusium. Then it divided and moved in one direction towards Alexandria and the rest of Aegypt [Egypt], and in the other direction it came to Palestine on the borders of Aegypt; and from there it spread over the whole world, always moving forward and travelling at times favourable to it.

Whatever the source, the bacteria arrived in Constantinople in 541, and people there immediately began to die. It spread quickly, moving as far north as Denmark and as far west as Ireland. In Constantinople even the emperor fell ill, though he survived. Most were not as lucky. More than five thousand people a day died at the height of the outbreak. Procopius described the horror:

> During that time it seemed no easy thing to see any man in the streets of Byzantium [Constantinople], but all who had the good fortune to be in health were sitting in their houses, either attending the sick or mourning the dead. And if one did succeed in meeting a man going out, he was carrying one of the dead.

PANIC IN THE STREETS

People in Constantinople took to wearing name tags when they went out. That way, if they dropped dead in the streets, their bodies could be identified.

The fleas that carry plague are usually less active in cold weather, so deaths began to lessen as winter approached. Over the next seven decades, though, the disease recurred again and again. By the time the outbreak ended, at least 25 million people had died, though it is impossible to find an exact number. Half of Europe's population was gone. The disease recurred periodically for the next three hundred years, though never to such a degree. Although the Plague of Justinian was devastating across the known world, there were not many records of it. By the 1300s, few people were aware that the Plague of Justinian had ever taken place.

ROOTS OF THE BLACK DEATH

We do know about one effect of the Plague of Justinian, however. The bacteria *Yersinia pestis* had made its way into central Asia. There it stayed, enzootic, in the tarabagan population of the remote Mongolian steppe. But as the centuries passed, these desolate areas saw more and more human activity.

By the 1300s, the Mongols held a huge empire that stretched from Siberia and China to the Persian Gulf. They were great warriors, and they were also merchants. They controlled the overland Silk Road, which ran from China in the east to the Black Sea in the west. Traders carried spices, porcelain, silk, gems, carpets, and foods along the route, which passed through the Mongolian steppe and the Gobi Desert. The merchants and armies that moved along the route brought grain with them, and their grain attracted black rats. Very possibly the travelers disrupted populations of tarabagans. The tarabagans' fleas leaped onto the travelers' rats, and the plague leaped with them.

In the 1320s, the plague moved into populated areas of China, causing an outbreak that killed relentlessly. By the end of the decade, millions of Chinese had died. India too may have been hit hard, though there are no records of the number who died. The plague marched through Persia, Mesopotamia, Syria, and Egypt.

This undated Chinese silk painting shows a caravan transporting ceramics along the Silk Road. Behind the cart stand other people from the ceramics business, including customs agents, craftspeople, bodyguards, and even bandits hiding in the hills.

Caffa, on the shores of the Black Sea, had been settled by the merchants of Genoa. They wanted an outpost from which they could ship their Silk Road goods to the harbors of Europe. Although known for their conquests in war, the Mongols had given the town, originally a fishing village, to the Genoese to increase their trade outlets. Surprisingly, the Mongols had allowed the town to remain in Italian hands.

Over the years, Caffa had grown and prospered. By 1346 it was a city-state with a population of more than seventy thousand.

In the nearby town of Tana, a street fight broke out one evening between a group of Mongols and some Genoese merchants. Words and then blows were exchanged. When it was over, a Mongol had been killed. Immediately, the Mongols organized and attacked the Italian population of Tana in revenge. The Italians fled to the walled city of Caffa. The Mongols, also known as Tatars or Tartars, followed and laid siege to the city. The siege went on

A portrait of a Mongol from an Italian painting of around 1336

BLACK DEATH

The term *Black Death* was not used to describe plague until the 1600s, when there was another outbreak in England. Some reports claim the name arose because bleeding beneath the skin was so great in septicemic plague that it made victims' limbs look black. Others say the term came into use because some plague sufferers' tongues turn black. Still others believe it came from the Latin words *atra mors*, which were used to describe the plague. *Atra mors* means "terrible death" or "black death."

for a year. Gabriele de Mussis, a lawyer from Piacenza, Italy, described what happened next:

> But behold, the whole army was affected by a disease which overran the Tartars and killed thousands upon thousands every day. . . . All medical advice and attention was useless; the Tartars died as soon as the signs of disease appeared upon their bodies: swellings in the armpit or groin caused by coagulating humours [thickening body liquids], followed by a putrid fever. . . . The dying Tartars . . . ordered corpses to be placed in catapults and lobbed into the city in the hope that the intolerable stench would kill everyone inside. What seemed like mountains of dead were thrown into the city. . . . No one knew, or could discover, a means of defence.

The Genoese quickly threw the decomposing bodies into the sea, but it was too late. Their fleas and the disease they carried remained behind in the city of Caffa, where they could hitch a ride westward to Europe.

CHAPTER THREE
DEATH SAILS IN

They died by the hundreds day and night.
I, Agnolo di Tura, called the Fat, buried
my five children with my own hands.

—*Agnolo di Tura del Grasso, Siena,*
fourteenth century

It was a warm, early October day in 1347 when a fleet of twelve Italian ships entered the harbor of Messina in Sicily. The three-masted caravels, trading ships owned by merchants of Genoa, came from Caffa. The busy harbor rang with the shouts of workers who gathered at the docks, ready to board the incoming ships and unload the spices, silks, and porcelain that had come from the Far East. But the men soon noticed that something was wrong.

36

The ships appeared nearly deserted. Their sails flapped limply in the autumn wind. Onlookers could see only one or two men on each ship, not the dozens needed to ready the ships for docking. One caravel seemed to have no one on board at all. Gradually the bustle of the harbor quieted, until the land was as still as the ships at sea. Confused, the Messinians watched as a small rowboat was lowered from the lead ship, and two men climbed in and began to row to shore. As they approached, a murmur rose up from the waiting crowd. Those in front saw it first—the men's necks had huge black swellings, and their faces were pale and sweating. One was covered by small red sores. Their eyes were glazed with pain and fever. They staggered out of their boat, and a path opened for them as people fell back in fear and confusion, not wanting to touch the men.

Others clambered off the ships, and all seemed ill. The dockworkers had never before seen a sickness like this. Nervous and fearful, they decided that they would wait to unload the cargo.

Within days, many of the dockworkers had been stricken with high fever and excruciatingly painful swellings. As Michele da Piazza, a Messinian friar (monk), later reported, "The Genoese carried such a disease in their bodies that if anyone so much as spoke with one of them he was infected with the deadly illness and could not avoid death." In terror, the people of Messina converged on the docks and demanded that the ships leave. Those sailors still alive set sail wearily to look for a harbor that would take them in, but it was too late for Messina—and for the rest of the continent. The bubonic plague had arrived in Europe.

This Italian illustration from the 1500s shows sufferers of the bubonic plague.

PLAGUE IN SICILY

As people in Messina began to realize that a disease unlike any other had broken out, they reacted with panic. Many fled the city, some of them already sick and dying. They went to the nearby town of Catania, and the people there let them in and nursed them. Before long, the Catanians too were infected, and the disease began to spread quickly throughout the island. Then people on other islands around the Italian peninsula became infected: on Sardinia, then Corsica, and then Elba. Those who remained in Messina turned against one another in fear, as Friar Michele da Piazza reported:

It bred such loathing that if a son fell ill of the disease his father flatly refused to stay with him, or, if he did dare to come near him, was infected in turn and was sure to die himself after three days. Not just one person in a house died, but the whole household, down to the cats and the livestock, followed their master to death.

THE MAINLAND IS STRICKEN

The plague reached the Italian mainland in a matter of weeks. There were several avenues of entry for the disease. The Genoese vessels that had been chased out of Messina went up the coast, stopping at ports and leaving sickness in their wake. Other ships from Caffa sailed up the east side of Italy, taking plague to the canal city of Venice. Sicilians rushed to the mainland, desperate to escape the death that stalked them. It seems likely that all three forms of the plague were present. Descriptions from the time are vivid. Some, like Gabriele de Mussis's, noted symptoms of bubonic plague:

> First, out of the blue, a kind of chilly stiffness troubled their bodies. They felt a tingling sensation, as if they were being pricked by the points of arrows. The next stage was a fearsome attack which took the form of an extremely hard, solid boil. In some people this developed under the armpit and in others in the groin. . . . As it grew more solid, its burning heat caused the patients to fall into an acute and putrid fever.

Others, like Michele da Piazza, described what sounded like pneumonic plague:

> Breath spread the infection among those speaking together, with one infecting the other, and it seemed as if the victim was struck all at once by the affliction and was, so to speak, shattered by it. This shattering impact, together with the inhaled infection . . . so

infected and invaded the body that the victims violently coughed up blood.

And the writer Giovanni Boccaccio may have been referring to septicemic plague when he wrote, "Later on, the symptoms of the disease changed, and many people began to find dark blotches and bruises on their arms, thighs, and other parts of the body, sometimes large and few in number, at other times tiny and closely spaced."

By January of 1348, plague had broken out in Venice and in Pisa, the port closest to Florence. Merchants quickly brought it overland and up the River Arno into Florence, the jewel of the Italian mainland.

Florence in the 1300s was a center of art and literature. It was the home of Dante Alighieri, who wrote *The Divine Comedy: Inferno*, *Purgatorio*, and *Paradisio*, and the celebrated artists Giotto and Cimabue. It was renowned for its architecture—the famous Ponte Vecchio (a bridge across the River Arno) and the magnificently striped Duomo, or cathedral, that was still being built. Despite its wealth, however, Florence had suffered a famine the year before, which killed as many as four thousand people. Bread was still being rationed throughout the city. Many Florentines were weakened by the famine and were completely unable to fight off the disease. It swept through the city with astonishing speed.

The Florentine historian Marchione di Coppo Stefani described the effects of the plague in his beloved city:

In the year of the Lord 1348 there was a very great pestilence in the city and district of Florence. It was

of such a fury and so tempestuous that in houses
in which it took hold previously healthy servants
who took care of the ill died of the same illness.
Almost none of the ill survived past the fourth day.
Neither physicians nor medicines were effective. . . .
There was such a fear that no one seemed to know
what to do. When it took hold in a house it often
happened that no one remained who had not died.
Dogs, cats, chickens, oxen, donkeys, sheep showed
the same symptoms and died of the same disease. . . .
Frightened people abandoned the house and fled to
another. Those in town fled to villages.

The numbers of dead were nearly incomprehensible.
Florence was one of the most densely settled regions in
Europe in 1347. In months the plague took fifty thousand of
its inhabitants—over 50 percent. So many were dead, no one
knew how to dispose of the bodies. Stefani, an eyewitness,
reported on the horror:

At every church, or at most of them, they dug
deep trenches, down to the waterline, wide and
deep, depending on how large the parish [church
community] was. And those who were responsible
for the dead carried them on their backs in the night
when they died and threw them into the ditch, or
else they paid a high price to those who would do
it for them. The next morning, if there were many
[bodies] in the trench, they covered them over with
dirt. And then more bodies were put on top of them,

with a little more dirt over those; they put layer on layer just like one puts layers of cheese in a lasagna.

Giovanni Villani, a Florentine merchant, had been writing a history of the city for his entire life. He had compiled twelve volumes about Florence's art and literature, the glory of its architecture, and the nobility of its citizens. In 1347 he began describing the famine and earthquakes that had rocked northern Italy. He turned his pen to the plague in 1348. The last line he ever wrote was, "And the plague lasted until . . . " He stopped his chronicle there, intending to fill in the date when the disease had run its course, but he never wrote another word. He too had become one of the plague's victims.

By April or May, the important hill town of Siena had been hit. Agnolo di Tura del Grasso, a Sienese, wrote, "It was a cruel and horrible thing. . . . It seemed to almost everyone that one became stupefied by seeing the pain." As the weather warmed, towns and cities succumbed, until the entire peninsula had been engulfed by the disease.

THE GREAT COUNCIL TAKES ACTION

Some of the towns and cities began to take steps to try to control the epidemic. Venice was the first to respond. The Great Council, which ruled the city, organized a committee to create the first modern public health policy. The committee ruled that all ships coming into Venice must be searched and those with dead aboard were to be burned. The committee shut down the inns and taverns where people gathered. It

When the plague reached Siena, a group of monks led by Bernard Tolomeo (front right, with red scarf) devoted themselves to caring for the sick. This Italian painting from the 1600s honors their work.

required the prompt removal and burial of the dead onto outer islands. Nevertheless, about 60 percent of the population perished. Because so many had died and public morale had sunk so low, the committee forbade the wearing of mourning clothes in an attempt to build hope and bolster confidence.

The council in Florence required Florentines to get rid of all bodies and the clothing and bedding of those who had died of plague. It barred visitors from Pisa and Genoa from entering the city. By summer, though, four hundred people a day were dying in Florence. Bells usually were rung to announce a death, but so many people were dying that the city banned the tolling of bells. Florence became eerily quiet as the number of dead continued to rise. In nearby

Pistoia, too, city officials prohibited the tolling of bells, but they went even further. The Council of the People in Pistoia set forth a series of laws called Ordinances for Sanitation in a Time of Mortality, which included such rules as these:

> The bodies of the dead shall not be removed from the place of death until they have been enclosed in a wooden box, and the lid . . . nailed down so that no stench can escape. . . .

> When someone dies, no one shall dare or presume to give or send any gift to the house of the deceased, or to any other place on that occasion, either before or after the funeral, or to visit the house, or eat there on that occasion. . . .

> No one shall dare or presume to raise a lament or crying for anyone who has died outside Pistoia.

Milan went still farther in its civic response. Whenever plague was found in a household, the house itself was walled up, with the living as well as the dead and dying trapped inside.

Eventually, though, the city governments could do no more. The Great Council of Venice gave up and even threw open the doors of Venice's prisons, advising the inmates to flee. The council members in Florence died, leaving the city leaderless. All over Italy, people were left to fend for themselves.

Citizens of Venice carry the bodies of plague victims out of the city in this Italian illustration from the 1300s. Workers at the right bury the dead as a bonfire destroys corpses.

"SOME FLED TO VILLAS, OTHERS TO VILLAGES"

The earliest and most common reaction to the plague was flight. The Messinians had fled from it in Sicily, and the Italians continued to try to find a safe haven where the plague could not follow. As Stefani reported, "Child abandoned the father, husband the wife, wife, the husband, one brother the other, one sister the other. . . . Some fled to villas, others to villages in order to get a change of air. Where there had been no [plague], there they carried it; if it was already there, they caused it to increase."

By summer of 1348, there was nowhere left to flee. People stayed where they were. In Florence some people hoped that quiet, clean living would save them, as writer Giovanni Boccaccio described:

> Wherefore they banded together, and, dissociating themselves from all others, formed communities in houses where there were no sick, and lived a separate and secluded life, which they regulated with the utmost care, avoiding every kind of luxury, but eating and drinking very moderately of the most delicate viands [foods] and the finest wines, holding converse with none but one another, lest tidings of sickness or death should reach them, and diverting their minds with music and such other delights as they could devise.

Others began holding elaborate dinner parties in an attempt to enjoy themselves fully before almost certain death. Marchione Stefani told how "men gathered together in order to take some comfort in dining together. And each evening one of them provided dinner to ten companions and the next evening they planned to eat with one of the others. And sometimes if they planned to eat with a certain one he had no meal prepared because he was sick. Or if the host had made dinner for the ten, two or three were missing."

As much of the population died, however, some of those who survived prospered. Among these were apothecaries (druggists), those who carried away the dead (the *beccamorti*), the greengrocers who sold herbs used to fight the infection, and physicians, surgeons, and barber-surgeons.

MEDIEVAL MEDICINE

Italy in the fourteenth century had several medical schools. One at Salerno, founded in the ninth century, is considered to be the first modern European medical school. Students at Salerno studied for seven years and then practiced for a year with another physician. Before they were admitted to the physicians' guild, ten judges examined the students in Latin. The judges then had to vouch for their learning and morals. Physicians were on a social level with wealthy merchants and were much respected. They usually treated their patients at their homes. Only those who had no money for a doctor or who were dying went to hospitals.

A doctor takes a patient's pulse during a home visit. This image comes from a medical manuscript from the 1300s.

The study of medicine in the Middle Ages did not focus on human anatomy and the way disease spreads. Most medical schools forbade human dissection on religious grounds, and physicians knew nothing about infectious disease. Medical students based their work on that of earlier physicians. These included the Greek physician Galen, who practiced in the second century, and the Persian physician Abu Ali al-Husayn ibn Addallah ibn Sina, known as Avicenna, who lived from 980 to 1037. Galen theorized that the human body consisted of four fluids, or humors: blood, phlegm, black bile, and yellow bile. Each humor corresponded to a temperature and a condition of moisture: blood was hot and wet, phlegm was cold and wet, black bile was cold and dry, and yellow bile was hot and dry. A physician's job was to try to maintain balance among the four humors to promote health. Illness was an imbalance, and a doctor had to prescribe a food, drink, or herbal blend that would restore balance. Physicians believed that most plants and liquids had properties that corresponded to the four humors. Their prescriptions were carefully planned to raise or lower the levels of the unbalanced humors.

Avicenna's contribution to medieval medical theory was an encyclopedia of medicine, a collection of all the medical knowledge of the Arab world. His *Canon of Medicine* was an influential text from the twelfth to the sixteenth century, and it linked the study of medicine to astrology. Physicians influenced by his writings saw the universe as a system that had a strong effect on the systems of the human body. They held that Earth was fixed in the center of the universe, and

THE BODY AND THE ZODIAC

Doctors believed that a region of the body corresponded to each sign of the zodiac, as shown below. Surgeons were advised not to treat these areas in people born under each sign.

Aries: the head
Taurus: the neck and shoulders
Gemini: the arms and hands
Cancer: the chest
Leo: the heart
Virgo: the intestines
Libra: the kidneys
Scorpio: the genitals
Sagittarius: the hips
Capricorn: the legs
Aquarius: the knees
Pisces: the feet

seven planets circled it. The stars they also saw as fixed and unmoving, creating a circle that was divided into twelve parts, the twelve signs of the zodiac. As the planets moved through the signs, they affected humans in various ways.

While physicians studied the theories of medicine available at the time, surgeons did the hands-on work of trying to cure the sick. They were the social equals of notaries and goldsmiths. Surgeons were rarely university educated, though they were literate (could read and write), and they were considered second-tier members of the physicians' guilds. Many physicians disdained surgery. Often it was nothing more than bloodletting, cutting a vein to release excess blood to restore the balance of humors, though some surgeons performed more specialized and elaborate procedures.

Below surgeons were barber-surgeons, who were often illiterate. They also bled patients, sometimes using bloodsucking worms called leeches to draw out blood. They might also try cupping. In this procedure, they placed heated glass cups on a patient's skin to draw the blood to the surface.

A physician opens a patient's vein with a small knife while the patient holds a bowl to catch the blood. This image illustrates a medical book made in Florence in 1356.

Sometimes they placed the cups over a cut vein. At other times, they put them on uncut skin to draw out poison through the pores. Most often, cupping was used on women, children, and the elderly.

Physicians believed that once the plague had entered the body, it created poison that moved through the body. The body tried to move the poison away from the heart, where it would kill the victim. It collected in one of three places: behind the ears, in the armpits, or in the groin. This belief corresponded with the places where buboes appeared, reinforcing the idea. Physicians felt that a bubo was the body's attempt to get rid of the poison and could be a good thing, especially if it burst.

HOW TO BLEED A PATIENT

One of the major medieval health texts from the University of Salerno was the *Regimen Sanitatis Salernitanum*, or *Salernian Regimen of Health*, which offered this advice on bleeding patients.

Practice phlebotomy [bleeding] at the beginning of acute and very acute illnesses.

Take a lot of blood from those of middle age;

From children and older persons take only a little.

Take twice as much blood in spring, but only the normal amount in other seasons.

A physician lances (cuts open) a plague bubo on a woman's neck in this French painting from the mid-1300s. Behind her, other patients wait for treatment, pointing to their sores.

Most people, physicians included, believed that disease was at least in part the result of sin—a punishment from God. They saw the plague as a punishment for the sins of an entire community. Prayer was the first line of defense, and it was always a doctor's first recommendation. Physicians did advise other ways to avoid the plague, however. Many of them believed that the plague was carried in bad air and entered the body through the nose, mouth, or pores of the skin, and preventives focused on purifying the air. People burned sweet-smelling woods, such as pine and juniper, or herbs such as mint and marjoram. They carried clumps of herbs and aromatic substances that they kept near their mouths and noses. Other preventives included charms such as Bible verses, vials of holy water, gems, or even dried toads and hares' feet worn on the body. People also carried relics, or items associated with a saint and assumed to be holy. They hoped that the saint would protect the wearer.

Physicians advised people to stay away from damp places and bad smells and to avoid physical exertion or strong emotions. They urged moderation in diet, with no spicy foods or moist foods, such as milk or fish. Stefani reported that "all fruits with a nut at the center, like unripe plums and unhusked almonds, fresh broadbeans, figs, and every useless and unhealthy fruit, were forbidden." But still people took ill from plague. When they did, physicians were helpless. Physicians who didn't flee or die—for physicians were more likely than anyone to be exposed to plague and to die from it—would prescribe herbs and send for the barber-surgeon to bleed and cup their patients, trying to restore the balance of humors. Their efforts were usually useless, but there was very little else a physician could do.

CHAPTER FOUR

THE SOUTH FALLS

> The deadly plague reigned everywhere, and
> once populous cities, because of the death of
> their inhabitants, now kept their gates firmly
> shut so that no one could break in and steal the
> possessions of the dead.
>
> —*from the chronicle of the monastery of
> Neuberg, Austria, ca. 1349*

As plague infiltrated the Italian mainland, the Genoese merchant ships that had been chased out of Messina continued to spread death. They docked at the port city of Marseilles, France, in November 1347. The people of Marseilles, recognizing that the caravels carried a fatal disease, quickly forced them to set sail again, but as in Messina, it was too late. Reports later claimed that fifty-six thousand died in Marseilles. Then the plague moved inland.

The disease approached Avignon, the home of the pope, in March 1348. Avignon, once a small, sleepy town in southern France, had become one of the great cities of Europe. The papal palace, erected when the church's administrative power moved from Rome early in the 1300s, was at its center. It was a huge building of stone walls and turrets, with many kitchens, dining halls, and luxurious bedrooms. Around it stood bishops' palaces and the houses of papal clerks. But as the twisted streets ranged farther from the palace, the thin-walled homes of the city's poor pressed more tightly together. Like other European cities, Avignon was dirty and crowded. It was ripe for the rapid spread of disease.

Construction of the papal palace in Avignon began in 1335, under Pope Benedict XII. The next pope, Clement VI, expanded the palace and filled it with beautiful works of art.

The papal court was soon aware of the approaching pestilence. Pope Clement VI had four doctors, and they recommended that he seat himself between two huge fires in his bedroom. This, they felt, would purify the air that the pope breathed, cleansing it of disease. The pope at first agreed, but when he saw the extent of the devastation in his city, he took action. He ordered processions of devotion in which worshippers walked through the city praying. Thousands in Avignon joined them to appeal to God to lift the plague from the city. The processions grew larger and the participants more desperate. Clement soon realized that the frantic marchers could cause a riot, and he stopped the processions. He was powerless to do much else. Louis Heyligen, a musician who worked for Cardinal Giovanni Colonna, described the devastation in Avignon: "To be brief, at least half the people in Avignon died; for there are now within the walls of the city more than 7000 houses where no one lives because everyone in them has died, and in the suburbs one might imagine that there is not one survivor."

The pope purchased a new cemetery for Avignon, but it quickly filled. When all the burial grounds in the city were full, Pope Clement consecrated the Rhone River, making it a holy place to lay the dead. Families floated the bodies of their dead kin down the river, and this stream of corpses flowed slowly to the Mediterranean Sea.

As the plague moved relentlessly toward Paris, King Philip VI commanded the medical faculty of the University of Paris to find out what was causing the disease. As the Italians had done, the French doctors turned to the skies and to the ancients to look for causes. In their report, they wrote their findings:

We say that the distant and first cause of this pestilence was and is the configuration of the heavens. In 1345, at one hour after noon on 20 March, there was a major conjunction of three planets in Aquarius. This conjunction, along with other earlier conjunctions and eclipses, by causing a deadly corruption of the air around us, signifies mortality and famine.

The Paris physicians went on to explain that the planets Saturn and Jupiter had come together in the sky, signaling great events and the death of large numbers, and that because Mars was aligned with them, a "great pestilence" was created "in the air." Just as the signs of the zodiac regulated different zones in the human body, so too the placement of planets within the constellations affected human life as a whole. In the medieval study of astrology, Mars was seen as a negative planet, associated with war. It tended to stir up violence and death. Saturn, too, was a planet of bad influence. While Jupiter was seen as the best planet, its power and position relative to the other planets at the time did not allow its influence to overcome that of the other two.

The doctors went on to suggest various ways to prevent and treat the disease. French doctors lanced and cauterized (sealed with heat) the buboes. That only succeeded in creating infection and spreading the disease. Later, in 1365, John of Burgundy, a French physician, wrote a treatise on the prevention and cure of plague, drawing on his experiences decades before. To prevent plague, he recommended inhaling aromatic spices during the colder months. He went on to say:

If, however, the epidemic occurs during hot weather it becomes necessary to adopt another regimen, and to eat cold things rather than hot and also to eat more sparingly than in cold weather. . . . You should use cucumbers, fennel, borage, bugloss [a common plant] and spinach, and avoid garlic, onions, leeks and everything else which generates excessive heat.

If the patient became ill despite these actions, John called for a diet of "small scaly fish" eaten with "barley water or small ale." He also recommended a protective covering made of herbs, to be placed directly on the buboes, claiming it "draws the venomous matter to itself, coagulates it and mortifies it."

Nothing helped, of course. Paris lost as many as fifty thousand people. Many small French villages simply disappeared as their inhabitants ran away or died.

STOPS ALONG THE WAY

As the French died by the tens of thousands, plague was making its way through other countries and onto other continents. Ships from Caffa had gone not only to Messina in Sicily and on to France but to Greece, Constantinople, and to Alexandria, Egypt. The plague hit those areas hard and spread inland. In the Middle East, Palestine, Syria, and the cities of Baghdad and Mecca suffered in 1347 and 1348. In Africa, the region that is present-day Libya and the cities of Tunis and Cairo were hit by the plague in 1348. Cairo, in particular, suffered terribly. In late summer, about three hundred people died each day. By October the death count was three thousand a day. In December the plague suddenly worsened. Modern scientists think it may have mutated into a pneumonic form. Suddenly, ten thousand to twenty thousand people were dying each day in Cairo. Funerals took place around the clock. At the biggest city mosque (Islamic house of worship), a double line of coffins stretched out the door. Later, bodies were simply thrown in alleys or tossed into the Nile River. Nobody knows how many millions died in all.

THE IBERIAN PENINSULA

Plague came to the Iberian Peninsula from Marseilles aboard a ship, as was so often the case. It struck Granada with such force that, according to some reports, the Moors of Granada considered converting to Christianity in the hope of stopping the spread of the disease. Quickly, though, it became clear that Christians were dying of plague in numbers just as great. In general, the Muslim response to plague was somewhat different from the Christian response. Though both religious traditions believed the disease came from God, Muslims did not believe it was a response to human sin. They felt it was simply God's will, and so they did not flee from it. They believed they would enter paradise after death as a reward for their suffering.

The disease was well established throughout Iberia by April 1348. In June it appeared in Santiago de Compostela, a town in northwestern Spain, just north of Portugal.

Santiago de Compostela was and still is a pilgrimage site, declared a holy place for Catholics by papal decree in the eleventh century. It was second only to Rome and Jerusalem as a destination for religious pilgrims, who came to pray to the bones of Saint James. James was reputed to have preached in Spain, and his bones are said to be buried in the cathedral at Santiago de Compostela. During the Middle Ages, thousands of pilgrims walked to the site every year to show their devotion. Many of them came hundreds of miles on foot across the mountains dividing Spain and France. Traffic to Santiago de Compostela increased enormously during the plague years, as pilgrims tried to purge the sins they believed had caused the disease. When the plague

ON PILGRIMAGE

Medieval pilgrims were easily recognizable to those along the way. They wore wool robes and round felt hats. They carried staffs with a hook on which they could hang a water flask and a bag of possessions. Pilgrims going to Jerusalem, the holy city in the Middle East where Jesus preached, wore crosses on their robes to honor his crucifixion. Those going to Rome were decorated with a pair of crossed keys, representing the keys to the kingdom of heaven. Those heading to Santiago de Compostela had cockleshells *(right)* sewn around the brims of their hats to represent the cockles, small shellfish, found on the beach where Saint James's body was brought ashore in Spain.

reached Santiago, those same pilgrims contracted it and carried it back to their homes or died of it on the way.

DEATHS GOOD AND BAD

The Alps, which separate Italy from much of the rest of Europe, were no match for the plague. In 1348 the disease crossed over the mountains into Germany at the same time that it moved eastward from France. Huge death tolls resulted: six thousand dead in the town of Mainz, eleven thousand in Munster, and twelve thousand in Erfurt. Meanwhile, the plague moved from Venice to southern Hungary. Its march was relentless, and Europe was utterly powerless to stop it. People began behaving strangely as they frantically tried to find both a cause and a cure for this onslaught.

As the death toll from the plague mounted in 1348, people throughout Europe turned more and more to religion. To the medieval Christian, death was the result of sin. Before Adam and Eve sinned by eating the forbidden fruit in the Garden of Eden, death had been unknown to humans. Their sin had brought death into the world. A good death was vitally important if the individual was to reach the heaven that Christ's death had made possible for humankind. A treatise written in the Middle Ages explains the good death:

for a Christian man to die well and surely it is necessary that he knows how to die; as a wise man says: "To know how to die is to have a heart and soul ever ready to go Godwards." . . . Therefore every man, not only religious but also every good and devout

Christian man that desires to die well and surely, ought to live in such wise and so behave himself always that he may safely die at whatever hour God wills.

Although death often came early and suddenly in medieval Europe, few people, if any, lived a life without sin and were entirely ready for death. So it was vitally important that a dying person receive the Catholic sacraments of confession and last rites shortly before death, so as to be free from sin. As the plague raged, however, achieving such a carefully planned death became virtually impossible. Priests died in such numbers that not enough were left to administer last rites. Many of those who survived were afraid to enter the homes of dying plague victims. And death often occurred so quickly that there was no time for these rites. Pope Clement VI tried to address this problem by creating a special Mass intended for turning away plague while also making it easier to enter heaven if the illness struck. The pope

granted 260 days of indulgence [freedom from purgatory] to all penitents, being truly contrite and confessed, who heard the following mass. And all those hearing the following mass should hold a burning candle while they hear mass on the five following days and keep it in their hand throughout the entire mass, while kneeling; and sudden death shall not be able to harm them."

This decree soothed some, but others were too desperate for such official comfort. Many became more humbly spiritual, giving up all excesses in food, drink, and behavior. Some chose to follow the way of Saint Francis of Assisi, a thirteenth-century Italian friar known for his humility and simple spirituality. Others reacted in the opposite way, eating, drinking, and carousing in an effort to enjoy earthly pleasures to their fullest before they died.

THE JEWS BECOME SCAPEGOATS

As terror and confusion reigned on the continent, the people looked for a scapegoat—someone to blame. For centuries Jews had been persecuted in Europe. Many Christians considered Jews to be the killers of Christ. They feared and resented Jews for their refusal to accept the teachings of the Catholic Church. Jews had been despised, restricted, and murdered in many countries and city-states. Officially the church protected them because, as Pope Clement said, "we are . . . mindful that Our Savoir chose to be born of Jewish stock when he put on mortal flesh for the salvation of the human race." But unofficially, Christians considered Jews the enemies of Christianity and blamed them for illness, bad luck, and even bad weather. Jews had been accused of murdering children and poisoning food throughout the thirteenth and the beginning of the fourteenth centuries. In the 1200s, the Viennese were forbidden to buy meat from Jews because it might be poisoned.

The king of England expelled all Jews in 1290, and the king of France did the same in 1322. Elsewhere in Europe, they were forbidden to work in most governments, to fight in the army, to own land, or to work as artisans. One of the very few occupations left to them was that of moneylender. Lending money and adding interest on the loan amount was forbidden to Christians under church law. As moneylenders charging interest, some Jews grew very wealthy, and this wealth served to increase Christian resentment against Jews. Christian attacks on Jewish communities were common in the 1100s and 1200s. Widespread outbreaks of violence against them occurred in 1321. Then the plague arrived.

In this scene from a Jewish synagogue (place of worship) in northern Spain, a reader on a raised platform leads worshippers. The painting appears in a Jewish book of worship from around 1350.

THE CHURCH AND USURY

The practice of usury is charging interest for lending money. Interest is the percentage the lender charges the borrower and is the source of the lender's profit. It was forbidden by the Catholic Church because of the many bans on it in the Old Testament (the first books of the Bible). These bans began in the Book of Exodus 22:24: "If thou lend money to any of My people, even to the poor with thee, thou shalt not be to him as a creditor; neither shall ye lay upon him interest" and went on through Deuteronomy, Ezekiel, and Proverbs. Many Jewish scholars interpreted these sanctions to mean that Jews could not charge other Jews interest on a loan, but they could charge those who were not Jewish. Muslims were prohibited from the practice as well.

As plague attacked Spain and France, whispers immediately started about poisonings of wells and of the air by Jews. In part, these rumors spread because many Jews did not use water from the common wells of towns and villages. They may have been aware that the water in those wells was unclean. Herman Gigas, a German Franciscan friar, recorded how the Jews confessed to poisoning water: "And many Jews confessed as much under torture that they had bred spiders and toads in pots and pans, and had obtained poison from overseas, and that not every Jew knew about this wickedness, only the more powerful ones, so that it would not be betrayed."

Communities rose up against their Jewish residents, and the attacks quickly multiplied. In France and Spain, townspeople tortured and killed hundreds of Jews in pogroms, or attacks targeted specifically against Jews. Germans and Swiss murdered hundreds more. One incident, in which a Jew named Agimet of Geneva was tortured until he confessed, was recorded by a historian of the time, Jacob von Konigshofen.

> Agimet the Jew, who lived at Geneva and was arrested at Chatel, was there put to the torture a little and then he was released from it. And after a long time, having been subjected again to torture a little, he confessed in the presence of a great many trustworthy persons. . . . Agimet took this package full of poison and carried it with him to Venice, and when he came there he threw and scattered a portion of it into the well or cistern of fresh water which was there near the German House, in order to poison the people who use the water of that cistern.

In Basel, Switzerland, citizens rounded up the whole Jewish population and burned them to death in a pogrom. In Strasburg half the Jewish community was burned alive—nearly a thousand men, women, and children—and the other half was banished. Appalled, Pope Clement issued a bull (decree) against persecution of the Jews, pointing out that the plague "has afflicted and afflicts the Jews themselves." He said to the clergy,

Angry Christians burn alive a group of Jews during an outbreak
of the plague in Flanders (part of modern Belgium) in 1349. The
painting illustrates a history of the plague written around 1352.

We order . . . that each of you . . . should straitly
[immediately] command those subject to you . . .
not to dare (on their own authority or out of
hot-headedness) to capture, strike, wound, or
kill any Jews or expel them from their service . . .
and you should demand obedience under pain of
excommunication [banishment from the church].

King Pedro IV of Aragon, one of the few European rulers
who allowed Jews to work in his government, also spoke out,
ordering authorities to protect the Jews. But these efforts
could not stem the fear that fed the violence.

CHAPTER FIVE
THE PLAGUE RACES NORTH

And there was in those days death without sorrow,

marriage without affection, self-imposed penance,

want without poverty, and flight without escape.

—*John of Redding, 1300s*

England in the mid-1300s was flush with its recent successes in the Hundred Years' War. In 1346 the English army had invaded France. Soldiers carried longbows, a powerful kind of weapon, instead of bulky crossbows. The longbow could be fired rapidly, while the crossbow had to be cranked after each shot. A group of soldiers with longbows could shoot ten to twelve volleys of arrows per minute.

At the village of Crécy, King Edward III set up camp

and waited for the French king Philip's men to approach. With their longbows, the English archers could reach their opponents long before the French were in range to fire. This advantage allowed them to thin their enemy's ranks before hand-to-hand combat with swords began. Some reports claim that King Edward also had cannons, an innovation developed with the recent appearance of gunpowder. Gunpowder had been invented in China and arrived in England sometime

At the Battle of Crécy, English soldiers with longbows (right) attack French forces (left). The French soldiers at the lower left are loading and firing crossbows, which are powerful but slower to shoot.

in the 1300s. If the English army did use gunpowder and cannons, they fired small stones from them. The stones would have done little harm, but the French would have been terrified by the noise and the flames of explosions.

The hail of arrows loosed by the English longbows resulted in huge numbers of dead. More than fifteen hundred French knights and lords fell on the battlefield of Crécy—a tremendous victory for the English. King Edward went on to capture the French port city of Calais. When he returned to England in the fall of 1347, cheering crowds welcomed him with great fanfare. His victories brought riches to England, and Calais gave the English an entry port on the European continent for trade. It also gave the plague a means of access into England.

THE PLAGUE INVADES THE BRITISH ISLES

The earliest plague deaths recorded in England occurred in June 1348, in the port town of Weymouth. As ships from France sailed into the coastal cities and towns, plague spread along the English coast. Other ships brought it up rivers into the interior of the island nation. The city of Bristol in the southwest was hard hit in late summer. By fall the disease was closing in on London.

King Edward continued to rule England with a steady hand as the plague crept ever closer. Then, in early September, he received shocking news about his fifteen-year-old daughter, Joan. She had recently left England for Spain to marry Prince Pedro, son of the king of Castile. In

This 1348 engraving shows the arrival of the plague in England. On the left, a plague-stricken man begs for help. On the right, people flee their town, which burns behind them.

Bordeaux, France, Joan and her attendants stopped their journey because the plague was racing through the city. On September 2, the English princess died of the disease. Her body was never recovered. Some reports claim she was buried in the cathedral at Bordeaux, but more likely her body was burned. The mayor of Bordeaux decided to set fire to the port area to stop the spread of the disease. The fire, however, got out of hand and burned the castle where Joan had died. Devastated, King Edward wrote to King Alfonso of Castile:

> We are sure that your magnificence knows how, after much complicated negotiation about the intended marriage of the renowned Infante Pedro, your eldest son, and our most beloved daughter Joan, which was designed to nurture perpetual peace and create an indissoluble union between our royal houses, we sent our said daughter to Bordeaux, *en route* for your territories in Spain. But see (with what intense bitterness of heart we have to tell you this) destructive Death (who seizes young and old alike, sparing no one, and reducing rich and poor to the same level) has lamentably snatched from both of us our dearest daughter (whom we loved best of all, as her virtues demanded).

ROYAL PLAGUE VICTIMS

Most rulers in Europe survived the plague because of better food and living conditions. In fact, only one king, Alfonso of Castile (the English princess Joan's father-in-law-to-be), died of plague in 1350. It happened while he was besieging the Muslim stronghold of Gibraltar, Spain. Other royal deaths included Princess Joan; Eleanor of Aragon; and King Magnus of Sweden's two brothers, Hakon and Knut.

In England the upper classes died of plague in much smaller percentages than the lower classes. Estimates suggest that about 27 percent of upper-class English—the landed gentry who lived on their own ancestral property—died, while between 40 and 70 percent of peasants died. In part, a higher percentage of peasants died because they had poorer diets and health and lived closer to one another. Another factor was that in England, the houses of the nobility tended to be constructed of stone rather than wattle and daub, making it more difficult for rats and their fleas to enter.

Another group that died in huge numbers in England was the clergy. In Bristol, for example, ten out of eighteen local clergy died —a rate of over 50 percent—while only fifteen of the fifty-two city councilors (about 30 percent) were felled. Village priests were infected as they administered last rites, while monks, living closely together in less than sanitary conditions in monasteries, perished by the thousands. In Westminster Abbey alone, twenty-seven monks died in a matter of weeks. Two archbishops of Canterbury died in quick succession. By 1349 the shortage of priests to hear confession had become dire. The bishop of Bath and Wells issued a proclamation to his remaining clergy:

> We order and firmly enjoin you, upon your obedience, to make it known speedily and publicly . . . to everybody, but in particularly to those who have already fallen sick, that if when on the point of death they cannot secure the services of a properly ordained priest, they should make confession of their sins,

A priest blesses monks stricken by the plague in an illustration from an English encyclopedia from around 1370. Many monks died while caring for plague victims.

according to the teaching of the apostle [Paul, an early church leader], to any lay person, even to a woman if a man is not available.

King Edward was by then fully aware of the extent of the horror facing his kingdom. He resolved to keep the courts open, though, and he continued to tax his people to support the war effort. In one instance, he sent seven tax collectors to one area before one survived long enough to collect what was owed. But the king took the precaution of canceling the meeting of Parliament in 1349, and in January, he left London himself to take shelter in the countryside. In a letter to his bishops in 1349, he made it clear that he believed the plague was the result of sin:

> Since there is nothing that prayer cannot achieve when accompanied by entreaty [plea], humility, fasting, and the other defences of virtue, we have come hastening back devoutly to the weapons of prayer, humbly commending us and our people to the divine mercy. . . . For we hope that if, by God's grace, the people drive out this spiritual wickedness from their hearts, the malignancy [harmfulness] of the air and of the other elements will also depart.

Death continued to move steadily through England. In East Anglia, the most populous part of the island, over 50 percent of the people died. To make matters even worse, the weather all over England was terrible in 1349. Rain fell almost continually during the summer and fall. Herds of cattle and sheep, already neglected by farmers who were dead, dying, or fleeing the plague, were infected with diseases of their own that worsened in the dampness. Rinderpest, a contagious viral disease of cattle, and liver fluke, a parasitic disease of sheep and goats, raged through the herds. They died by the thousands and were left to rot in the fields.

The plague moved north, hitting the city of York in May 1349. Farther north, on the border with Scotland, an army of Scots had massed. They had heard of the devastation taking place throughout England. They thought that if they invaded England, the English would be helpless to defend themselves. Plague attacked first, though, and the Scots fled in terror, taking the disease back home with them.

At the same time, Y. *pestis* traveled west into Wales and across the Irish Sea to Ireland. Its effects were not well documented in either area. However, one Irish friar, John Clynn, wrote about the plague in the city of Dublin. He explained that many believed that the plague was the beginning of the Apocalypse, the end of the world as described in the Bible. In Ireland thousands made a panicked pilgrimage to Tech-Moling on the River Barrow to wade in what was considered holy water. They hoped their devotion would spare them in the coming days of death and horror. Despite this precaution, thousands perished. As John Clynn reported, "In Dublin alone 14,000 people died between the beginning of August and Christmas."

ONWARD TO SCANDINAVIA

From England, ships brought plague to Norway in 1348. Though much of Scandinavia was thinly populated, the disease spread from village to village with such speed and ferocity that modern scientists believe that the Scandinavian form of plague was probably pneumonic. As in other places, small villages were completely wiped out. One such village, Tusededal, had only one survivor, a small girl. When rescuers finally found her, she had become so wild that they named her Rype, or "wild bird."

A funeral procession follows the draped body of a plague victim into a Norwegian cemetery in 1349. At the church door, a priest tends to sick and grieving townspeople.

Iceland, then a colony owned by Norway, was one of the very few parts of Europe that was untouched by plague. Reports claim that a Norwegian merchant ship was loaded with goods and ready to sail from Bergen to Iceland in 1349, at the height of the outbreak in Norway. However, the sailors on board became ill and died, and the ship never sailed. No other ship from Norway went to Iceland that year, so the small island was spared. The island of Greenland was not as fortunate. Reports claimed that every person in Greenland died from plague. Denmark and Sweden were hard hit too. Sweden's King Magnus ordered his people to fast on Fridays, eating nothing but bread and water, and to walk to church barefoot on Sundays. Like Edward of England, he assumed that the plague must be a divine punishment for human sinfulness. He hoped that extreme forms of spiritual atonement would help bring it to an end.

THE HOLY ROMAN EMPIRE

In the Middle Ages, modern-day Germany, Austria, Belgium, the Netherlands, Switzerland, the Czech Republic, Slovakia, and northern Italy were part of what was called the Holy Roman Empire. The empire was ruled by an emperor, usually a German, who was crowned by the pope. During the plague, the Holy Roman Emperor was Charles IV. His far-flung empire was little more than a collection of villages and small cities, and his rule had little effect on the lives of the common people, who spoke different languages and

Gravediggers bury plague victims in the Flemish city of Tournai. The painting comes from a 1352 book by a monk named Gilles de Muisit, who survived the first outbreak of plague in Flanders.

lived by their own traditions. He was powerless to mount any resistance against the invader Y. *pestis*.

The plague had come over the Alps from Italy to Austria in the fall of 1348. It had spread throughout Austria by 1349. It had also crept steadily up the Rhine River toward Germany. In the spring of 1349, ships from both England and Norway landed in northern Germany with plague aboard. From south, north, and west, plague leaped into Germany with devastating effect.

The Germans reacted with the same terror as other Europeans. The inhabitants of the town of Lubeck, where nine thousand people died, became crazed with fear. They collected all their belongings and brought them to the local churches and monasteries. They believed that by giving up their worldly goods, they might save themselves. The monks and priests were afraid that the people's belongings might carry the plague, so they refused to accept them. Furious and terrified, the citizens threw their money and goods over the walls of the church property.

Fear led many to flee, leaving their possessions behind and their homes open and unguarded. One German chronicler wrote that in Lubeck, wolves roamed in packs at night, going into open houses and tearing children from their mothers. Other towns suffered similarly. In Hamburg 60 percent of the people died, and in Bremen, 70 percent perished.

THE FLAGELLANTS

In Dresden, Germany, in 1349, the plague approached rapidly. The townspeople were filled with fear. There was no escape. They had heard stories of other towns laid waste by the terrible disease, and they cowered inside their houses, praying and hoping to be spared.

Suddenly, the people of Dresden heard singing—men's voices raised in a hymn. They peered out from their homes and saw an eerie sight. A procession of men dressed in white robes and hoods, each marked with a red cross, marched two by two to the church at the center of town. They entered, and the people crept out to see what they would do.

After a short time, the group came out again. Then they stood in a circle. They stripped to the waist and fell to the ground. One man raised the whip he carried in his hand and went from one prostrate figure to the next, beating each. The townspeople gasped in shock as they watched the blood begin to flow, staining the white robes as red as the cross that decorated each one. Dresden was witnessing the movement called the Brethren of the Cross—the flagellants.

Flagellation, or whipping, had been a religious practice for hundreds of years. Groups of flagellants would wander from town to town, stopping at local churches, whipping themselves, and praying. Usually the flagellants were men, but occasionally women followed behind. The whipping was intended to echo the beating that Christ suffered on his way to crucifixion.

The Brethren of the Cross strengthened in Germany in the late 1340s. They took this practice of spiritual purification to its limits. They hoped that their reenactment of Christ's atonement for human sin would spare them from the curse of the plague.

To spare themselves from the plague, the Brethren of the Cross would stop at a plague-stricken town and whip themselves and one another. The painting comes from a Flemish manuscript from the mid-1300s.

To join the Brethren, members needed the permission of their husband or wife. They had to make a full confession of every sin they had committed since the age of seven. Then, for thirty-three and a third days, a number that corresponded to the number of Jesus' years on Earth, they walked from town to town, engaging in a frenzy of self-mutilation. They did not bathe, sleep in a bed, or converse with members of the opposite sex. In each town they reached, they would walk to the church, pray, walk out to the town square, and fall to the ground, where they then whipped themselves or one another. The monks of the monastery of Neuberg in Austria described the phenomenon.

Men gathered together from cities and towns
and went devoutly in procession from church to
church, walking two by two, totally naked except
for a white cloth covering them from their loins
to their ankles, singing beautiful hymns in honour
of the Passion in their mother tongue and beating
themselves so hard with knotted whips that drops
of blood spattered the roadway.

Before long the groups consisted of hundreds of Brethren,
presided over by one called the Master. He would whip them
as they fell to the ground, rose up, and fell again. Watching,
the townspeople would collect the blood in flasks, which
were considered to be holy relics. The people believed that
the blood, purified by pain, could protect them from death.

Within months the Brethren of the Cross had spread
across Europe. Officials at the University of Paris wrote to
Pope Clement, claiming that the movement was on the
verge of becoming a form of public hysteria that the church
would not be able to control. In a papal bull, the pope

PAPAL BULLS

A papal bull is a formal proclamation issued by the pope. The word
bull comes from the Latin word *bullire,* meaning "to boil." It is so
named because the seal on the proclamation, made of lead or gold,
looked like a bubble in boiling liquid. The seal shows the saints
Peter and Paul and has the name of the pope who issued the bull.

condemned the movement, but the Brethren would not cease their flagellation until the plague itself had ceased.

Some reports of the time claimed that the Brethren who wandered through the streets of the Holy Roman Empire were violently anti-Jewish. As the lines of white-robed Brethren approached a town, the Jews would flee or go into hiding. If any were found, the flagellants would kill them and destroy their homes.

THE PLAGUE COMES FULL CIRCLE

To the east of the Holy Roman Empire lay Russia, bordering central Asia, where the plague had originated. Medieval Russia was not a unified country but a collection of principalities and one large city-state, Novgorod. The people in the north were Christian, but they were members of the Russian Orthodox Church, a branch of Christianity that had its roots in the Byzantine Empire. In 1054 the Eastern Orthodox Church, based in Constantinople, had split from the Western, or Roman, Church. The Russian Orthodox Church developed from the Eastern Orthodox Church. Until the fifteenth century, it was headed by the Patriarch of Constantinople, not the pope in Rome.

The Mongols, led by their khan, had swept through Russia in the 1230s. They were known as the Golden Horde for the yellow color of the khan's flag and trappings. All the Russian principalities had fallen to them except Novgorod. It was spared only by the death of the khan. The Russian towns and cities paid tribute to the Mongols, led by the next khan, Janibeg, but the Golden Horde did

Simeon Ivanovich became grand prince of Moscow in 1340. He supported the Golden Horde until he and two of his sons died of the plague.

not stay in the north to watch over their territories. They preferred the south. So over time, the cities in the northeast began to acquire some independence. Gradually, during the thirteenth and fourteenth centuries, the Russian city of Moscow became more powerful. The city still paid tribute to the khan, but the Mongols gave the ruler of Moscow the title of grand prince.

Khan Janibeg's army was the one that had laid siege to the merchant city of Caffa in 1347, flinging the plague-ridden bodies of dead soldiers into the walled city and starting the pandemic that laid waste to much of the world. But the plague did not move directly from the areas around Caffa into Russia. Tensions within the Golden Horde and between the Mongols and the Christians of northern Russia had virtually stopped trade between north and south. During the time that the Mongols suffered from the plague, they weren't sending infected traders and goods north. Instead, four years later, having ravaged the rest of Europe, Y. *pestis* headed eastward and southward into Novgorod and the city of Pskov. Known by the Russians as the *mor zol*, the "evil plague," it reached Moscow in 1352. There, it killed thousands, including the grand prince.

The Russians had no way of knowing it, but this was the Black Death's last gasp. In 1353 the deaths began to slow and, finally, they came to a halt. More than five years had passed since the first ships from Caffa had docked in Sicily. In every conceivable way, the world had changed forever.

CHAPTER SIX
A DEVASTATED WORLD

A remarkable thing was noticed for the first time: that everyone born after the pestilence had two fewer teeth than people had had before.

—*John of Redding, 1300s*

At last it was over. Europe reeled, its death toll almost unimaginable. No one knows, even in modern times, how many actually died. In the 1300s, people had no idea of the size of Europe's population, and they had no way to measure the effects of the plague. One chronicler of the time estimated that nine out of every ten people died. Another claimed that three-quarters of the population died. Still another gave the number as four-fifths of the population.

Pope Clement's agents estimated the total number of dead at 23.8 million.

COUNTING THE DEAD

Historians have tried to come up with a reliable number of plague victims using records of all sorts, but every method they use has proved problematic. Tax rolls and rent records included only those who owned or rented land, so the number of poor peasants and serfs who perished could not be counted. Parish and village records were often incomplete and usually counted only the number of households, or hearths. It was impossible to determine the number of people in each hearth. A hearth that was abandoned at the time of the plague might have been deserted as the result of its inhabitants fleeing the area, not dying. Some historians have looked at bishops' registers. They have tried to determine the number of deaths in the general population from the number of clergy who died, but clergy often died in greater numbers than the general population. Some have looked at burial sites, but plague deaths resulted in many mass burials, so those interred could not be counted.

Until very recently, historians accepted the idea that between 30 and 45 percent of Europe's people perished. Then Ole Benedictow, a history professor at the University of Oslo in Norway, began looking at a combination of records. He came up with numbers, published in 2005, that appear to be the most reliable available. He estimates that before the plague, the population of Europe was around 80 million. In Spain, he claims, the plague reduced the population from 6 million to around 2.25 million. That means that 60 to 65 percent of the people died. In Italy he estimates that the death toll was between 50 and 60 percent. In France 60 percent were victims of the plague. In England about 62 percent of the population perished. He calculates that a total of 50 million people perished—60 percent of the total population of Europe.

Other historians maintain that there were lower numbers of victims—from 30 to 50 percent of the populace. There is no way to find a definitive number. We can only say with certainty that between one-third and two-thirds of Europe's inhabitants died.

The death toll was much higher among certain groups. The poor, who lived amid dirt and squalor and generally had worse health, died in greater numbers than the wealthy. Women also died at higher rates than men. Women spent more time indoors, close to rats and their fleas, while men spent much of their time working outdoors in the fields, away from Y. pestis. It appears that any woman who contracted plague while pregnant would die, as would her unborn offspring. Professor Benedictow points out that children's survival depended in part on which parent survived. If the mother died and the father lived, 90 percent of their offspring would die. If the father died and the mother lived, 70 percent of the children would die. If both parents survived, only 23 percent of the family's children would die. These numbers imply that a child's survival was very dependent on the care given by his or her mother—care that very likely led millions of women to contract plague from their sick children.

Death, in the form of a skeleton, takes a child from his parents with no warning. This image is part of a series created in Germany in the early 1500s, after a new outbreak of the plague.

The plague took a very high number of the clergy and doctors—those who were most likely to come into contact with the ill and dying. And surprisingly, it struck down a high number of those between the ages of twenty and sixty, seemingly in the prime of life and at their peak of health and strength. But those people were the same group who had been starved as infants and young children in the Great Famine, when their immune systems were developing. Though it seemed that they should have been able to survive if anyone did, they carried a hidden weakness that often proved fatal.

Asian records have not been studied in depth, but tens of millions certainly perished. Mortality in the Middle East was a little lower. Scholars estimate that fewer than one-third of the population of the Middle East died, though reasons for this lower death toll are unclear.

The plague left behind a lopsided world. There remained a relatively high percentage of the very young and very old still living and a low percentage of women. Not many priests and doctors were left to aid those still alive, and too few peasants remained to work the land and grow the food the survivors needed.

Considering these factors, it is easy to understand that the population did not recover quickly. In addition, the plague recurred nearly every decade until the 1400s, so the population continued to drop for over a hundred years. None of the later outbreaks was nearly as devastating as the first, probably because the weakest and most susceptible members of the population had already died. Still, Russia did not achieve pre-plague population numbers until 1500, while Norway's population did not rebound until about 1650.

The plague continued to reappear at intervals in later centuries, but by the 1700s, it was no longer an epidemic. Why did it disappear? Some scientists believe that Y. pestis mutated into a less deadly form, but many consider this unlikely. Other scholars point out that the black rat was replaced in Europe by the larger and more adaptable brown rat. The brown rat was less likely to host the flea that carried the plague bacteria. Still others feel that improvements in hygiene and the use of arsenic as rat poison were responsible. Perhaps the disappearance of epidemic plague was a result of multiple factors.

Whatever the truth about the plague's victims and its end, this much is obvious: nearly every farm, manor, village, town, and city was profoundly affected. Those peasants who survived had lost family, friends, neighbors, priests, and overlords. Nobility who lived through the plague lost their servants and those who ran their businesses and farms. The plague rocked every aspect of society in ways that modern people can barely imagine. The world in 1353 seemed bleak indeed.

THE BLACK DEATH IN ART AND LITERATURE

Surrounded by death, the medieval mind had to find a way to understand and deal with what had happened. Nobles and peasants alike sought to understand God's reason for allowing the plague to rage. Some of these individuals tried to translate the terror and sadness into art. Many of those artists left alive created paintings and woodcuts that showed an angry God— or sometimes a demon or devil-like creature—hurling spears or shooting arrows of plague at towns and villages. Other artists turned to more religious themes, painting in a style less realistic and simpler than pre-plague artwork. Historians note that the change in style may have resulted from the widespread death of those painters who were better trained and more sophisticated in style and choice of subjects.

One of the earliest artworks that refers directly to the plague is a fresco, or painting on plaster, on the wall of a church in Lavaudieu, France. It is titled *The Black Death* and shows

In this wall painting from Perugia, Italy, an angel directs Death, a winged skeleton, to shoot townspeople with arrows representing the plague. Artist Benedetto Bonfigli painted it in 1464.

the figure of Death as a woman. In earlier art and literature, Fortune (a figure presenting the chances for the future) was often depicted as a woman. That this painting shows Death as a woman draws on the idea of chance in who would live and who would die. Death holds arrows in her hands, and the dead, shot through in the spots where buboes would have formed, lie at her feet. The victims include priests and peasants, rich and poor.

One recurring artistic theme that appeared at this time was the *danse macabre,* or dance of death. The idea of the danse macabre, which made its way into both art and literature, may have originated in an encounter between two monks and a group of dancers at the height of the plague. According to the story, when asked why they were dancing, the dancers replied that they believed that their dancing had thus far kept the plague from their town. They said they planned to continue dancing until the danger had passed completely. Danse macabre images usually depict a corpse or skeleton dancing with a member of one social class, leading members of other classes into the dance. The paintings often had several panels and featured twenty-four or thirty-six characters. These might include popes, cardinals, priests, emperors, kings, knights, merchants, peasants, and children. The danse macabre shows that nobody, no matter what social position, could escape the dance of death. The danse macabre first appeared as a fresco on a cemetery wall in Paris.

This French fresco is the first image of the danse macabre. Created around 1470, it shows people of all social ranks, including (from left to right) a lawyer, a musician, and a scholar, dancing with skeletons.

Another popular plague theme appeared in both art and literature. It was known as the three living meet the three dead. In this genre, three living people, often portrayed as young, wealthy, and well dressed, meet three corpses, who are depicted in various stages of decomposition. The message implied is "What we are now, soon you shall be." In verse each of the living figures comes away with a different lesson. One learns that the purpose of life is to prepare for the next, one learns to focus on the present, and one learns to give up all earthly pleasures.

In the wake of the plague, medieval artists were more and more aware of the briefness of life and people's inability to control their earthly destiny. The plague changed the way men and women thought about life, and it increased their preoccupation with death and the afterlife.

This fascination with death found its way, most naturally and most gruesomely, into the burial chamber itself. Before the plague, the tomb of a wealthy nobleman might be decorated with a statue of the man, lying peaceably in full armor, perhaps with a favored hunting dog at his feet. Post-plague tombs often still featured the peaceful nobleman lying as if asleep. Just beneath that statue, however, was a second statue, showing the dead man as a decomposing corpse or a twisted, terrifying skeleton. This image, again, was a reminder to the living that they too would end up like the dead man.

WRITERS AND THE PLAGUE

The earliest written works influenced by the plague were probably the medical treatises called *consilia*. Beginning in

1348, physicians investigated the nature of the disease and its symptoms, methods of prevention, and treatments. More than two hundred consilia were written in the fourteenth century. Most blamed bad air or sin for causing the plague.

Plague also found its way into poetry, drama, and fiction. The work of fiction best known for its treatment of plague is *The Decameron*, written by Giovanni Boccaccio in 1350. Boccaccio was writing in Florence, one of Europe's greatest cities and one of those hardest hit by the disease. He describes a group of young, well-to-do Florentines who, after going to the funeral of a plague victim, decide to flee the city for a country estate in the hills. There, they would "hear

Boccaccio's Decameron *inspired many artists to create works illustrating its stories. In 1483 Italian artist Sandro Botticelli painted this illustration of one of the tales, "The Story of Nastagio degli Onesti."*

birds singing . . . see fresh green hills and plains," and escape, perhaps, with their lives. Once in their country home, the young people pass the time by telling stories. Their tales form the bulk of *The Decameron*. Before beginning the main part of his work, however, Boccaccio devotes his introduction to a description of the plague and its effects, both physical and social, on Florence and its inhabitants. His descriptions are vivid, showing a city in panic, its social order breaking down. He tells how many people reacted by drinking and eating in excess. He writes that they "maintained, that to drink freely, frequent places of public resort, and take their pleasure with song and revel, sparing to satisfy no appetite, and to laugh and mock at no event, was the sovereign remedy for so great an evil."

Another Italian writer and friend of Boccaccio, the poet Petrarch, was deeply affected by the plague. In a work titled "Letters on Familiar Matters," written in 1350, he mourned, "Our former hopes are buried with our friends. The year 1348 left us lonely and bereft . . . there is just one comfort: that we shall follow those who went before." Many of Petrarch's greatest poems were addressed to a woman named Laura, who is traditionally identified as a French noblewoman named Laura de Noves. In May 1348, Petrarch received word that his beloved Laura had died of the plague. He immortalized her death in these lines from "On the Announcement of the Death of Laura":

> For you I still must burn, and breathe in you;
> For I was ever yours; of you bereft,
> Full little now I reck all other care.

With hope and with desire you thrill'd me through,
When last my only joy on earth I left—
But caught by winds each word was lost in air.

Petrarch's poems were
well known in Italy and
France, but most people
may have only heard them
recited aloud. They would
not have had access to them
as works to be read. Books
were painstakingly written
and copied by hand before
the invention of the printing
press in the 1450s. With the
printing press, books could be
printed by machine, making
them available to greater
numbers of people. Among
the earliest works printed
were *The Decameron* and the

An Italian painter created this
portrait of the poet Petrarch
in 1754.

poems of Petrarch. By the end of the 1400s, these and other
works dealing with the plague were circulated widely.

As plague continued to reappear at regular intervals, it
became a popular motif in drama and literature. William
Shakespeare refers to the disease in several of his plays,
including *Romeo and Juliet*. When Mercutio, Romeo's cousin,
is stabbed by Juliet's relative, he cries out, "A plague on
both your houses!" He is cursing both the Capulets, who are
Juliet's family, and the Montagues, Romeo's family. Later

in the play, Juliet, forbidden to marry her beloved Romeo, decides to take a potion that will make it seem as though she has died. She sends a priest to let Romeo know of her plan. The priest, however, comes into contact with a plague-infected family, and as he explains, "the searchers of the town,/suspecting that we both were in a house/where the infectious pestilence did reign,/Seal'd up the doors." Unable to escape, he misses his meeting with Romeo. Romeo, sure that Juliet is truly dead, kills himself. Juliet, when she wakes and finds Romeo dead, uses his dagger on herself. The plague, then, was at least partly responsible for the deaths of the two best-known lovers in English literature.

The English writer Ben Jonson, whose seven-year-old son died of plague in 1603, treats the disease in his play *The Alchemist*. Daniel Defoe, author of *Robinson Crusoe*, wrote *A Journal of the Plague Year* in 1722. His description of the 1665 plague outbreak in London reveals that the disease and people's reactions to it had not changed much over the three centuries since the earlier pandemic:

> So the Plague defied all medicines; the very physicians were seized with it, with their preservatives in their mouths; and men went about prescribing to others and telling them what to do till the tokens were upon them, and they dropped down dead, destroyed by that very enemy they directed others to oppose.

The London magistrates did what the city of Milan had done in 1348: that is, they shut up the families of plague

Citizens of London, England, bury victims of the plague of 1665. So many people died in so short a time that bodies were buried in mass graves without coffins or markers.

victims in their homes as soon as the disease made its appearance. Defoe describes one such family:

> The misery of those families is not to be expressed; and it was generally in such houses that we heard the most dismal shrieks and outcries of the poor people, terrified and even frighted to death by the sight of the condition of their dearest relations, and by the terror of being imprisoned as they were.

Each outbreak of plague, from the Black Death of 1348 to the Italian plague of 1629 to the Great Plague of London in 1665 to the 1771 Plague of Moscow, the last serious occurrence in Europe, resulted in an outpouring of plague-related pamphlets, books, plays, poems, and art. These works were an attempt by those surviving to understand what had happened and to record the suffering they had witnessed.

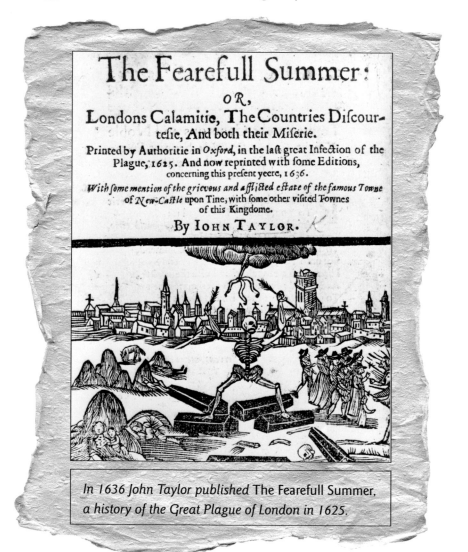

In 1636 John Taylor published The Fearefull Summer, a history of the Great Plague of London in 1625.

PLAGUE AND FIRE

The Great Plague of London raged from late 1664 to early 1666. It is estimated that it killed more than seventy-five thousand people. In September 1666, fire broke out in London and spread wildly, eventually burning over 80 percent of the city—thirteen thousand houses. Many historians believe that the fire, which killed many of the city's rats, helped end the plague.

Although we can still view the plague paintings and read the works that mention or focus on the pestilence, the Black Death did not truly change art or literature in any measurable or lasting way. The Renaissance, a movement in art, literature, and thought that began in Italy near the end of the fourteenth century and spread throughout Europe, transformed the post-plague preoccupation with human suffering and death into an inquiry into the nature and meaning of life. The real changes were found in the economies of Europe, in the nature of education and the spread of learning, and in the state and position of the Catholic Church, which was left to deal with a population halved by disease and burdened by years of suffering and terror.

A CHAPTER SEVEN
A NEW ERA BEGINS

Because a great part of the people, and especially of workmen and servants, late died of the pestilence, many seeing the necessity of masters, and great scarcity of servants, will not serve unless they may receive excessive wages.

—*Edward III*, Ordinance of Labourers, *1349*

Most of medieval Europe had been rural. The farming economy was based on the medieval feudal system of peasant and overlord, with class divisions deep and obvious.

As the plague passed through towns and villages, it destroyed the feudal system on which much of the European economy was established. With from 30 to 60 percent of the peasants and serfs dead, there was a serious shortage of workers, both in the manor houses and in the fields. Those landowners still alive desperately needed workers to plant and harvest, and to cook and serve. Before the plague, serfs had been forced to work for the lord of the manor, but afterward, they had the freedom to move to wherever workers were most needed and wages were highest.

PEASANT IN DEMAND

In Oxham, England, a plowman who made two shillings a year in 1347 made seven shillings in 1349 and ten shillings in 1351. Landlords lowered rents to attract workers. Landlords who couldn't find the employees to work their land and needed cash sold their land cheaply. Some peasants were able to buy land, and those peasants who already owned land increased their holdings. A new class of landowners grew up. Called yeomen in England, their place in the social order fell above the landless peasant and below the landed knight. They became a vital part of society.

In northern Italy, peasants refused to work on farms unless the landlords gave them a percentage of the crop. Peasants' incomes rose, while the incomes of the upper classes shrank, bringing the two groups closer together.

Skilled workers, too, were in great demand, and physicians, priests, and gravediggers, in particular, could ask for any payment they dared. The craft guilds had been devastated by the plague, and few skilled craftspeople were left alive to teach apprentices. Towns and cities, desperate for their services, offered carpenters, teachers, shoemakers, and metalworkers free housing and tax breaks.

PEASANTS VERSUS GOVERNMENT

Rising wages in England soon came to the notice of the king. In 1349 he issued an ordinance in an attempt to freeze wages to their pre-plague levels, stating that each worker should "take only the wages, livery [uniforms], meed [an earned reward], or salary, which were accustomed to be given the places where he oweth to serve, the twentieth year of our reign of England [1347]." The ordinance threatened that workers who charged too much would be "committed to the next gaol [jail]." Few officials were left alive to enforce the law, however, and wages continued to rise. In 1351 King Edward passed the Statute of Labourers, requiring workers to take an oath to charge only pre-plague fees for their services. By this time, it was possible to enforce the law to some extent, and some workers paid fines or received prison terms. In 1352, for example, seventy-five hundred people were fined in Essex County.

Growing peasant unrest because of these laws—and similar ones passed on the European continent—may have contributed to peasant revolts. Some were quite violent. The English Peasants' Revolt began in Essex in 1381, when peasants, unhappy with low wages, found a reason to rebel when the government suddenly tripled a tax levied on them. The revolt spread quickly throughout southeast England. The rebels, led by a man named Wat Tyler, marched on London, attacking manor houses and monasteries, burning homes, and opening prisons. They reached the Tower of London, took the archbishop of Canterbury from his rooms there and, recognizing him as a figure of governmental power, executed him. Not long after, the king's forces met Tyler's, and Tyler was pulled from his horse and killed. The peasants quickly dispersed, and the king

In this painting from around 1470, the mayor of London (left) attacks Wat Tyler at the order of King Richard II (center). King Richard appears again (right), giving orders to his army.

later had the leaders of the rebellion hunted down and killed. Similar uprisings took place in France in 1358 and 1381, in Florence in 1378, and in Ghent, Belgium, in 1379.

As wages rose, so did the prices of goods when tradespeople realized, because of greater demand, they could get more for their products. Wheat, meat, and cheese were more expensive all over Europe. Even so, workers earning more were able to afford more expensive food. People in general began to eat a more varied and healthier diet as the standard of living rose.

Fewer peasants available to cultivate farmland led to an increase in unused land. Many landlords, troubled by the rising price of farmwork, decided to convert their land to pasture and raise sheep. Especially in England, the very landscape of the countryside began to change. No longer surrounded by a patchwork of crops, villages were bordered by fenced-in meadow populated by herds of sheep. Sheep needed fewer workers to care for them, so towns and cities grew as the unemployed peasants moved to them in search of higher pay. Urban life began to take over what had previously been a mostly rural world. In northern Germany, for example, the large town of Lubeck had 422 new citizens in the year after the plague. Before the plague years, an average of only 175 moved there each year. In Luneberg the new citizens numbered 95, more than three times the pre-plague number.

Another effect of the labor shortage was the introduction of women into the workforce. Before the plague, peasant woman had labored in the fields and some women worked alongside their husbands in a family business. Afterward, women became metalworkers, clothworkers, and brewers. In fact, the brewing industry soon was run almost entirely by women. Women also ran the family shops that had once been the responsibility of their husbands and fathers. While women still had few rights under the laws of the land, they enjoyed greater personal power because they had more responsibility and more money.

Labor shortages required business owners to begin thinking in new ways. They had to find innovations that would allow them to produce goods with fewer workers. Dutch fishers, for example, developed a new way to use drift nets to catch large quantities of fish, which they would salt, dry, and store. This enabled them to stay longer at sea and bring back more fish—a necessity with fewer fishers left alive. Many mills were converted from processing grain to sawing wood. One of the greatest and most influential innovations was the invention of the printing press in Germany. Books became available to the masses—if only they could read.

In this German woodcut from 1568, two men operate a printing press. In the back, two more men set type for the next pages.

LEARNING AND THE NEW ORDER

As it did to other aspects of life in Europe, the plague devastated education. Four of the thirty existing universities had been forced to close because of the pestilence. The number of students enrolled at Oxford University, in England, dropped from thirty thousand before the plague to six thousand afterward. Teachers, many of whom were priests or monks, had died in huge numbers too. In France the students of Avignon complained to the pope that "the university body . . . is deprived of all lectures, since the whole number has been left desolate by the death from pestilence of doctors, licentiates [holders of a degree lower than a doctor] bachelors, and students." As a result, universities began training and hiring teachers who were not from the church. These secular (nonreligious) educators had not been trained in Latin as monks and priests were, so they taught in the vernacular, or local language. The universities in each country taught classes in the language of that country. Gradually, as the shock of the epidemic passed, new universities were founded in Vienna, Austria; Kracow, Poland; and Heidelberg, Germany. Oxford opened two new colleges, and Cambridge University opened four. The study of Greek language and learning, which would later flower in the Renaissance, grew popular. Medicine, in particular, underwent a great change. Because medical texts were being written in the vernacular, anyone who was literate was able to read them. Medicine was no longer accessible only to the most educated.

The study of anatomy, forbidden by the church and once pursued at least in quiet if not in secrecy, came out into the open. Anatomy was taught in most universities, and it included dissections. Students began to grasp more fully the workings of the human body. Previously, the understanding of anatomy had been based on the works of the ancient Greek Galen, who had performed dissections only on pigs, apes, and dogs. Beginning at the end of the 1300s and over

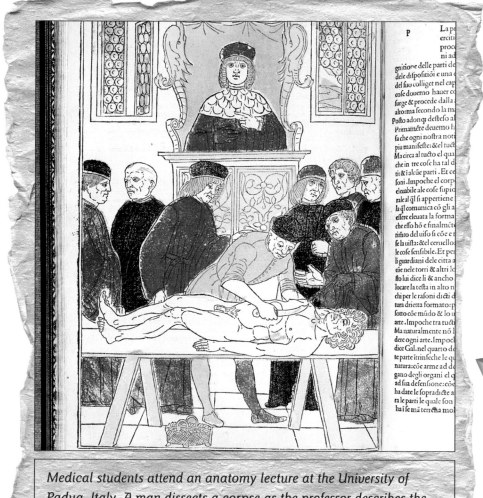

Medical students attend an anatomy lecture at the University of Padua, Italy. A man dissects a corpse as the professor describes the work. The image is from an Italian medical book from 1483.

As dissections became more common, finding fresh bodies for study became more difficult. Often students were required to obtain bodies themselves. Executed criminals were one common source, but some students robbed graves for their cadavers.

the next two centuries, physicians were increasingly able to see that the human body differed from those animals in certain vital ways. A book published in 1543 by Andreas Vesalius of the University of Padua, *On the Structure of the Human Body*, gave medical students accurate, illustrated descriptions of the inner workings of the body. Medical schools also added courses in pharmacy and medical botany.

Gradually, the distinction between physicians, who theorized about disease and prescribed mainly herbal remedies, and surgeons, who bled and cut their patients, began to disappear. Surgery became part of the university program. In many places, surgeons were required to acquire a university degree to belong to a guild. By 1400 educated surgeons were as respected as physicians.

RETHINKING DISEASE

During the plague years, physicians and others had begun to think in a different way about the origins of disease. The spread of the plague, as it raced through village, town, and city, seemed less and less like the result of bad air or an angry God. In places where plague had become pneumonic, people could see that it moved from person to person. It seemed to jump from one victim to the next as they touched or breathed on one another.

In the early 1500s, a physician named Girolamo Fracastoro, working at the University of Padua, began an intensive study of diseases. In his treatise *On Contagion and Contagious Diseases*, he theorized that diseases could be transmitted from person to person by tiny organisms. He believed microorganisms move among victims in three ways: by direct contact between people, by soiled clothing and other objects, and through the air. This theory of microorganisms and their role in the spread of disease was centuries ahead of its time. Because it was based on something nobody could see—the tiny organisms that later were identified as bacteria and viruses—few paid close attention to Fracastoro's ideas. It wasn't until the nineteenth century that Louis Pasteur and Robert Koch elaborated on the theory to create the modern understanding of germs and their role in disease.

While Fracastoro's theory did not produce immediate changes in the field of medicine, it had some impact on the way hospitals were run. The Catholic Church had been establishing hospitals in Europe since the 500s. Monks or nuns staffed them, and wealthy patrons donated money for their support. Physicians rarely visited these places, though surgeons sometimes did. Hospitals were intended to provide comfort and relief for the ill as they struggled on their own toward recovery or, more often, toward death. It was a rare patient who emerged from a hospital cured rather than in a coffin.

HOSPITALS AND THE HOLY SPIRIT

Medieval hospitals were always built with their doors facing in the direction of the Vatican in Rome, the home of the pope. This practice was intended to help the Holy Spirit, a spiritual force, enter the hospital to aid the sick.

During the plague, however, many of these hospitals were used to isolate plague victims. The idea of isolating the ill—keeping them together and away from those who were not sick—was a relatively new one. Only sufferers from leprosy had been isolated before this, and that was because of fear rather than any understanding of contagion. Many of these plague hospitals were terribly overcrowded with the sick and dying. One in Florence, which had 175 beds, had nine hundred patients. A pest house in Milan had fifteen thousand patients at one time. The hospitals and pest houses probably served to spread the plague among their inmates and those who treated them. However, by isolating the victims, they may have helped limit the spread of disease outside their walls.

Well after the plague, when people had begun to suspect that plague and other diseases spread from person to person, the sick were separated according to their ailments in hospitals. Fracastoro's theory provided a scientific basis for this practice of quarantine, whether those applying it understood the nature of contagion or not. Isolating the sick did help limit the spread of disease. Physicians began visiting hospitals and treating the ill. Gradually hospitals became more than just places to die. At the Hôtel Dieu in Paris, patients gave a donation to cover the costs of their stay. They were placed in a ward according to their illness and slept on straw mattresses with feather pillows. Usually at least two patients and sometimes as many as four shared a bed. The hospital provided weekly shampoos and had several bathtubs,

Enclosed beds with curtains line the grand hall of the Hôtel Dieu in Paris. A chair and table stand outside each alcove for patients to eat at if they can get out of bed. At the end of the room is the chapel.

showing an increased respect for sanitation. Physicians treated patients, and more and more often, they recovered from their illnesses.

CITIES TAKE CONTROL OF THE SICK

The idea of isolating the sick was the first advance in public health policy. During the plague, cities passed ordinances and created health boards to oversee public health. They passed laws concerning trade with areas where disease was evident and tried to regulate sanitation. They also established plague controls during later outbreaks, including enforced isolation of the ill and the building of new pest houses. In Italy health boards required that all deaths be recorded as a way to judge whether an epidemic was occurring. They used this information to set up quarantines when epidemic disease was suspected and thus keep the illness from spreading.

Local governments became involved with keeping streets and public areas clean. In London the city government hired street cleaners and arranged for citizen volunteers to watch over them to ensure they were doing their job. Though the link between dirt and disease was still unclear, it had become obvious that a cleaner city was a healthier city.

A WEAKER CHURCH

As the plague receded, it left behind a continent filled with Christians whose faith in God and in his representatives on Earth had been strongly shaken. The high percentage of priests' deaths compared to other deaths shows that they had more exposure to plague than other citizens. This statistic suggests that priests stayed in their parishes in large numbers to tend the sick, giving what comfort they could and administering last rites. However, many church officials did flee. Probably stories of priests who abandoned their congregations had a much more powerful effect on people than the knowledge that many had remained. The evidence that priests, like anyone else, could give in to their terror in the face of approaching death shattered the faith of many.

Because so many parish priests died or fled, the church needed to replace them as quickly as possible. With no one available to administer the sacraments, the church was in danger of losing its stronghold on the populace. Few educated, experienced clergy were left to take the place of the dead or missing. Instead, the church quickly recruited and elevated ignorant, untrained youths, bypassing the normal many months of training. These young priests knew they were invaluable. They often demanded and received large salaries and many benefits. Parishioners, already angry about the excessive wealth and splendor the church had displayed before the plague, saw this extravagance as another reason for resentment. The growing strain between worshippers and their priests led many to begin seeking a more personal relationship with God. They depended less on their priests and relied more on prayers aimed either directly to God or to saints as intermediaries on their behalf.

THE CULT OF THE SAINT

The use of saints as intermediaries became much more widespread during and after the plague. A saint could intercede with God on a worshipper's behalf, making it more likely that a prayer would be heard and answered. People prayed to different saints depending on their needs. Mary, the mother of Jesus, was the saint people turned to most often. They felt she would be most likely to have the ear of Christ and could do most to help them. Many other saints also became popular during the plague. Saint Sebastian, who lived in third-century Rome, was killed by arrows shot by Roman soldiers for revealing that he was a Christian. People in the fourteenth century saw the arrows that pierced him as the arrows of plague, because Sebastian's many wounds looked like plague sores. So they prayed to Saint Sebastian for protection from the disease. People also called on the saints Cosmos and Damian, the patron saints of physicians, in times of illness.

The saint most closely identified with the plague was Saint Roch. He was reputed to have been born in 1295 in France, supposedly with the mark of a red cross on his breast. When he reached adulthood, he gave away all his wealth to the poor and traveled to Rome. As he passed through Italy, he is said to have cured plague victims with his touch. In Piacenza he contracted plague himself. But according to legend, a dog licked his buboes and this miraculously cured him. Portraits of Saint Roch almost always depict him with a dog at his side.

The church, post-plague, was acutely short of money because most of its funds came from donations by the

THE BLACK DEATH

116

THE POWERS OF SAINT ROCH

Saint Roch *(below)* is also the patron saint of bachelors, diseased cattle, dogs, falsely accused people, invalids, people with knee disorders and skin diseases, surgeons, and tile makers. As a patron saint, he watches over and protects these groups.

wealthy or taxes on the general population, many of whom had died. To raise money, the church gave new importance to the sale of indulgences, which granted time off in purgatory. As people's incomes rose, sales of indulgences rose too. The church sent out indulgence sellers, some of whom made a profession of the selling of indulgences and kept most of the proceeds of the sales, though sometimes a portion of the money went to the local ruler. Sellers of indulgences, like the Pardoner in Geoffrey Chaucer's

This illustration of Chaucer's Pardoner, painted in England around 1405, shows his white bag of indulgences.

Canterbury Tales, often played upon the post-plague fear that death would strike quickly and unexpectedly while the victim was in a state of sin. Chaucer points out about the Pardoner that "his wallet lay before him in his lap, / Bretful [brimful] of pardon come from Rome all hot." Many saw this practice as corrupt, and disillusionment with the church grew. While faith was still strong, respect for the church and especially for its clergy waned. Some Catholics turned to more private forms of worship. The wealthy built family chapels, neglecting their parish churches. Other Christians joined lay groups, which worshipped without clergy.

Worshippers expressed the idea of a more personal relationship with God in the practice of good works. These were charitable actions and donations that could help the givers attain salvation. Donations to hospitals, both by the living and in the wills of the dead, rose enormously after the plague. Pilgrimages to holy sites, considered an individual good work, increased in the 1350s and 1360s to such an extent that guidebooks were published and tourist accommodations sprang up along the routes.

CANTERBURY TALES

Chaucer's *Canterbury Tales*, written in 1386, was the story of one pilgrimage to the holy site of Canterbury in England. One of the earliest and best-known works written in English, it tells of a group of pilgrims, representing all walks of medieval life, from the noble knight to the lowly miller, from the humble monk to the haughty prioress (leader of a nunnery). They have come together under the protection of Harry Bailey, their tour guide, to walk to Canterbury. Each pilgrim tells a story that reveals much about both the storyteller and the world the pilgrims live in.

HERETICS

Anger at the moral failings of the organized church led some to question its doctrine and practices. In the late 1300s, John Wycliffe, an English theologian, attacked the sale of indulgences and the practice of masses said for the dead. These masses were supposed to speed the soul's journey to heaven. He condemned the masses because, like indulgences, they could be bought. This only benefited the wealthy, and it led to corruption among church officials. The pope condemned Wycliffe, but Wycliffe continued preaching and went on to translate the Bible into English. The church also condemned his followers, known as Lollards, as heretics and forced them to go underground to protect their form of Christian worship.

Wycliffe's teachings influenced Jan Hus, a Czech reformer. Hus preached in the Czech language rather than church Latin. He was eventually condemned as a heretic and burned at the stake. The influence of Hus and Wycliffe was strong, however. They and other similar thinkers laid the foundation for what would later resurface as the Protestant Reformation. This movement away from the Catholic Church eventually resulted in a complete split and the rise of new forms of Christian worship.

THE BEGINNINGS OF MODERN EUROPE

The Europe that we know, with its countries defined by borders, led by bureaucratic governments, and based on a capitalist economy, had its roots in the post-plague era.

This page is from a Bible made around 1400, using John Wycliffe's English translation of the text. Wycliffe believed that people should be able to read the Bible without having to learn Latin.

The plague's effect on the rise of a middle class, the spread of education, and the weakening of the once-all-powerful church was instrumental in constructing this society. The sudden, shocking death of millions of people made the survivors question and then begin to change the feudal society that had existed for centuries. Bubonic plague, in a sense, woke a slumbering Europe. It forced its inhabitants to move—some in leaps and bounds, some staggering, and still others pushed forward—into a new age.

THE PLAGUES AMONG US

Ring around the rosy

A pocket full of posy

Ashes, ashes

We all fall down.

—*traditional rhyme*

Some historians believe that children began singing this nursery rhyme during or just after the London plague outbreak of the 1660s. The "ring around the rosy" supposedly refers to the rose-colored circular lesions that arise on the plague victim's body. The "pocket full of posy" is the sweet-smelling flowers or herbs that were thought to ward off the disease. "Ashes, ashes" might refer to the bodies of the dead that were burned during the epidemic or to the Great Fire that ended the outbreak. And "we all fall down" refers, of course, to death.

Just as "Ring around the Rosy" is still heard on playgrounds and in school yards every day, so bubonic plague too is still with us. Worldwide, one to two thousand cases are reported each year, with an average of fifteen a year in the United States. There are still epidemic outbreaks, usually linked to the presence of rats living in close quarters with people. While no cases of plague have been reported in Australia or Europe, recent outbreaks have occurred in Asia, Africa, South America, and North America.

In the United States, most plague occurs in two regions. One region includes parts of New Mexico, northern Arizona, and southern Colorado. The other covers parts of California,

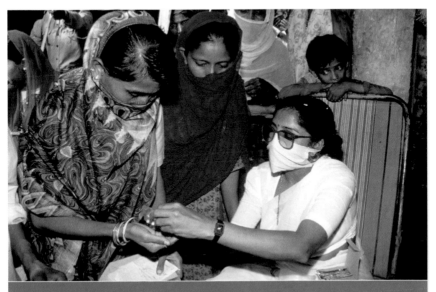

Residents of Surat, India, receive antibiotic pills after a 1994 outbreak of pneumonic plague. As many as one hundred people died before doctors stopped the spread of the disease.

southern Oregon, and western Nevada. The disease is enzootic
in wild rodents in those areas, especially in rock squirrels,
ground squirrels, and prairie dogs. As recently as May 2007,
a monkey at the zoo in Denver, Colorado, died of bubonic
plague. Scientists traced the monkey's illness and death to an
outbreak of plague in a nearby squirrel population.

Echoing the beginning of the outbreak of 1347, in August
2007, a fourteen-year-old Mongolian boy contracted plague
from a marmot he had hunted on the Mongolian steppe. The
boy had cut his finger while skinning the marmot, and the
disease progressed so rapidly that he died within four hours
of entering the hospital. The local authorities quarantined
(isolated) seventy-nine people with whom the boy had come
into contact, and the disease was stopped in its tracks.

In the twenty-first century, bubonic plague can be treated
with antibiotics. If treatment is started early, a cure is likely.
However, if plague spreads to the lungs, the death rate is
still over 50 percent. In areas of Africa, including Tanzania,
Kenya, Mozambique, and Botswana, where access to
antibiotics is limited, plague still occurs as an epidemic. As
a worldwide or even continent-wide killer, though, bubonic
plague is no longer a threat. The world is still threatened by
plaques though. Other diseases have taken the place of the
Black Death in recent times.

SPANISH FLU

In 1918 a form of influenza erupted among the soldiers
fighting in the trenches of World War I (1914–1918).
Called the Spanish flu, it spread quickly and brutally

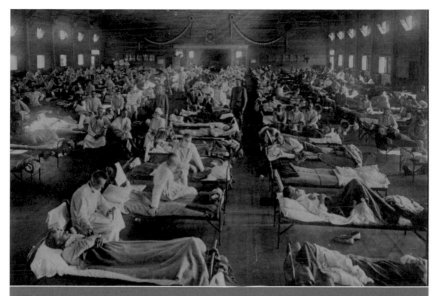

Soldiers suffering from the Spanish flu rest in an emergency hospital in Kansas in 1918. The flu weakened victims' immune systems, making them vulnerable to other illnesses as well.

around the world. For two years it raged, infecting one-third of the world's population, approximately 500 million people. Estimates of the dead range from 50 million to 100 million people. In terms of sheer numbers, the Spanish flu probably killed more people than the plague did. In terms of percentage of total population killed, however, its impact was much smaller. Still, since it affected nearly every country on Earth and spread so quickly and relentlessly, it reminded the world that epidemic disease was still with us.

HIV/AIDS

In 1981 the world felt the first hint of a new pandemic. U.S. hospitals began to report cases of a disease that appeared to break down the immune system, leaving victims helpless to fend off infection and other diseases. Eventually, scientists found the virus, human immunodeficiency virus (HIV) that causes acquired immunodeficiency syndrome, or AIDS. The virus, spread by contact with infected body fluids such as blood or semen, damages the immune cells that protect the body against infection. Though HIV is far more difficult to contract than influenza or plague, AIDS quickly became a pandemic. More than 25 million people have died of AIDS since 1981, and about 6,000 people are infected with HIV each day. In 2006 the U.S. government estimated that nearly one million Americans may currently be infected with HIV, with 25 percent of them not aware they have it.

HIV can be treated with a combination of medications, though it cannot yet be cured. Only a small percentage of those infected worldwide are able to get the drugs and medical care they need, however. This is because the disease is rampant in poor and developing countries, particularly in Africa and Asia, where people have less access to medical care and less money to buy medicine.

AVIAN INFLUENZA

Since the early 2000s, scientists have been talking about and studying avian influenza—the bird flu. This is a severe form of influenza that is found in some wild and domestic bird populations, mostly in Asia. The disease passes among birds, and it can infect humans who come into direct contact with sick birds.

In birds, avian influenza causes death in 90 to 100 percent of cases, often within forty-eight hours—similar to the statistics for pneumonic plague. However, for the disease to become a real threat to humans, the virus would have to mutate—to change its form—so it could spread easily from person to person. There have been a few cases of human-to-human spread, but these did not move outside family groups. Of those people who have come down with the disease, 60 percent have died.

There is no way to predict whether bird flu will become the plague of the twenty-first century. If it does, the bubonic plague has taught us much about how to avoid and contain epidemics. We know how disease is spread, and we know—in theory, at least—how to stop its spread. Scientists are working to develop vaccines—medications that help the body defend against a disease—to prevent the bird flu and other medications to lessen its impact. By looking back to 1347 and learning from the historical evidence, we can strive to avoid the devastation caused by diseases such as the bubonic plague, which echoes in even the most innocent-sounding nursery rhyme:

Ashes, ashes
We all fall down.

PRIMARY SOURCE RESEARCH

To learn about historical events, people study many sources, such as books, websites, newspaper articles, photographs, and paintings. These sources can be separated into two general categories—primary sources and secondary sources.

A primary source is the record of an eyewitness. Primary sources provide firsthand accounts about a person or event. Examples include diaries, letters, autobiographies, speeches, newspapers, and oral history interviews. Libraries, archives, historical societies, and museums often have primary sources available on-site or on the Internet.

A secondary source is published information that was researched, collected, and written or otherwise created by someone who was not an eyewitness. These authors or artists use primary sources and other secondary sources in their research, but they interpret and arrange the source material in their own works. Secondary sources include history books, novels, biographies, movies, documentaries, and magazines. Libraries and museums are filled with secondary sources.

After finding primary and secondary sources, authors and historians must evaluate them. They may ask questions such as: Who created this document? What is this person's point of view? What biases might this person have? How trustworthy is this document? Just because a person was an eyewitness to an event does not mean that person recorded the whole truth about that event. For example, a soldier describing a battle might depict only the heroic actions of his unit and only the brutal behavior of the enemy. An account from a soldier on the opposing side might portray the same battle very differently. When sources disagree, researchers must decide through additional study which explanation makes the most sense. For this reason, historians consult a variety of primary and secondary sources. Then they can draw their own conclusions.

The Pivotal Moments in History series takes readers on a journey to important junctures in history that shaped our modern world. Authors researched each event using both primary and secondary sources, an approach that enhances readers' awareness of the complexities of the materials and helps bring to life the rich stories from which we draw our understanding of our shared history.

STUDYING THE PLAGUE

A great many works have been written about the plague and its impact on society. Many draw on primary sources written in the fourteenth century. These include medical texts, legal and government documents, and church writings. None of these sources describing the catastrophe were written in the modern English that we speak and read. Most were in Latin. Modern readers would not be able to read even those that were written in the vernacular Italian, German, or English of the Middle Ages. These languages have evolved over the centuries and were very different in the 1300s. A U.S. historian studying a work about the plague written in 1348 in Italian, for example, would first have to translate the text into modern Italian and then into modern English. Even an

English text produced in the fourteenth century would have been written in what is called Middle English. This form of English was used between the eleventh century and the late fifteenth century. In making these translations, some details can become lost or confused, and different translators produce different versions of the same text.

Just as most of what we know about the plague has come through translation, so too many stories about its effects come through oral transmission. Historians also have to consider that most people writing in the 1300s did not know much about what was happening beyond the area where they lived. They knew their own village or town and perhaps had traveled to the nearest large town or city. They were often not aware of what occurred in the rest of the world. Writers who presented stories of events that took place elsewhere in the world were usually reporting spoken tales they had heard secondhand or even from third or fourth sources. It is likely that certain features of the original accounts were changed or omitted as they were repeated and passed from one person to another. The difficulties historians have had in gathering statistics on the plague are one example of this problem of full and reliable documentation. No one reporting at the time had complete knowledge of the extent of the plague and the deaths it caused.

Because so many original sources are available, however, historians have been able to put together a relatively complete picture of the plague and its effects throughout Europe. Their opinions on the impact of the pestilence differ. Some feel that it pushed Europe into the modern age, while others believe the impact was far smaller. This is a matter of historical interpretation. Each historian draws conclusions based on the information available. Each new work on the plague becomes a part of the body of scholarship that future historians must evaluate.

BOCCACCIO'S *DECAMERON*

Perhaps the most vivid and complete eyewitness picture of the effects of the plague on a specific time and place are found in the introduction to *The Decameron* by Giovanni Boccaccio, who wrote during the pestilence. This collection of stories was written in medieval Italian and set in Florence

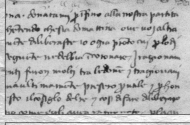

Boccaccio's young nobles flee Florence to avoid the plague. This image comes from an edition of The Decameron *that was copied by hand in Florence around 1370.*

in 1350, while the plague was raging in that city. It is framed by a fictional account of a group of wealthy men and women who flee from Florence to the nearby hill town of Fiesole. There they wait to see if the infection has followed them. They spend the time telling stories to one another over a period of ten days. To set up this group of tales, Boccaccio tells of the coming of the plague to Florence. He reports the rumors of how and where it started and describes its horrific symptoms. Although *The Decameron* as a whole is a work of fiction, the descriptions in the introduction give a vivid sense of the terror that the Florentines faced.

The beginning of the introduction reveals the way in which writers of the time, even those who attempted to write as eyewitness observers, had to rely on reports from others and on the beliefs and knowledge available. Boccaccio writes that the plague came from the East, which was a rumor at the time, although a true one. He also describes the forces that were believed to have caused the disease—the anger of God and the arrangement of the stars.

I say, then, that the years of the beatific incarnation of the Son of God had reached the tale of one thousand three hundred and forty-eight when in the illustrious city of Florence, the fairest of all the cities of Italy, there made its appearance that deadly pestilence, which, whether disseminated by the influence of the celestial bodies, or sent upon us mortals by God in His just wrath by way of retribution for our iniquities [sins], had had its origin some years before in the East, whence, after destroying an innumerable multitude of living beings, it had propagated itself without respite from place to place, and so, calamitously, had spread into the West.

Boccaccio goes on to describe the effects of the plague. He refers to rumors of symptoms in the East and explains how they differed from symptoms he saw in Florence. What is remarkable about this section of his introduction, however, is how its wording differs from translation to translation. Here is a version from a 1921 translation by M. Rigg:

Towards the beginning of the spring of the said year the doleful effects of the pestilence began to be horribly apparent by symptoms that shewed as if miraculous. Not such were they as in the East, where an issue of blood from the nose was a manifest sign of inevitable death; but in men and women alike it first betrayed itself by the emergence of certain tumours in the groin or the armpits, some of which grew as large as a common apple, others as an egg, some more, some less, which the common folk called gavoccioli. From the two said parts of the body this deadly gavocciolo soon began to propagate and spread itself in all directions indifferently; after which the form of the malady began to change, black spots or livid making their appearance in many cases on the arm or the thigh or elsewhere, now few and large, now minute and numerous.

133

Here is the same description, translated by John Florio three hundred years earlier, in 1620.

About the beginning of the yeare, it also began in very strange manner, as appeared by divers admirable effects; yet not as it had done in the East Countries, where Lord or Lady being touched therewith, manifest signes of inevitable death followed thereon, by bleeding at the nose. But here it began with yong children, male and female, either under the armepits, or in the groine by certaine swellings, in some to the bignesse of an Apple, in others like an Egge, and so in divers greater or lesser, which (in their vulgar Language) they termed to be a Botch or Byle. In very short time after, those two infected parts were growne mortiferous, and would disperse abroad indifferently, to all parts of the body, whereupon, such as the quality of the disease, to shew it selfe by blacke or blew spottes, which would appear on the armes of many, others on their thighs, and every part else of the body, in some great and few, in others small and thicke.

Some of the facts seem to be different in the two translations. In the first, Boccaccio appears to say that the disease began early in the spring and states that men and women in the West first showed signs of illness with gavocciolli (buboes). The second, earlier translation appears to state that the illness first showed up at the beginning of the year and that the swellings appeared only in children. The earlier translation gives the time as the beginning of the year because in Florence at that time, the year began on March 25, the feast day of Mary's conception of Jesus, so this fact is actually the same in both translations.

Boccaccio also describes the rapid, fearful spread of the plague and speculates on its origins and causes. At that time, of course, no one understood how the disease moved, which made its contagious nature all the more terrifying. Still, his account helped future historians and scientists to determine the type of plague that was devastating Florence based on its specific symptoms and form of transmission. Boccaccio observes this movement in detail without grasping the science behind it:

Moreover, the virulence of the pest was the greater by reason that intercourse [meeting together] was apt to convey it from the sick to the whole, just as fire devours things dry or greasy when they are brought close to it. Nay, the evil went yet further, for not merely by speech or association with the sick was the malady communicated to the healthy with consequent peril of common death; but any that touched the cloth of the sick or aught else that had been touched or used by them, seemed thereby to contract the disease.

Boccaccio goes on to describe an incident that illustrates vividly how sudden and shocking the disease could be.

So marvellous sounds that which I have now to relate, that, had not many, and I among them, observed it with their own eyes, I had hardly dared to credit it, much less to set it down in writing, though I had had it from the lips of a credible witness. I say, then, that such was the energy of the contagion of the said pestilence, that it was not merely propagated from man to man but, what is much more startling, it was frequently observed, that things which had belonged to one sick or dead of the disease, if touched by some other living creature, not of the human species, were the occasion, not merely of sickening, but of an almost instantaneous death. Whereof my own eyes (as I said a little before) had cognisance, one day among others, by the following experience. The rags of a poor man who had died of the disease being strewn about the open street, two hogs came thither, and after, as is their wont, no little trifling with their snouts, took the rags between their teeth and tossed them to and fro about their chaps; whereupon, almost immediately, they gave a few turns, and fell down dead, as if by poison, upon the rags which in an evil hour they had disturbed.

Although Boccaccio takes pains to explain that he saw this event with his own eyes, it is unlikely that it happened as he describes. It is possible that pigs could get plague, but they would not die within minutes of transmission. Either the writer is exaggerating what he saw or he is describing a tale told to him by someone else—or perhaps the pigs were infected earlier.

These selections illustrate the difficulties historians face in using narratives such as Boccaccio's. They must take into account how the times affected the way the writer perceives facts and details. Historians must be aware of the way in which different translators interpret the same words in different ways. Finally, historians must ask how the writer came by the information and how reliable it is.

TIMELINE

A.D. 541   The Plague of Justinian begins.

1330s   Bubonic plague surfaces in China.

1337   The Hundred Years' War begins.

English archers (left) *attack French forces* (right) *during a battle of the Hundred Years' War (1337–1453).*

1346   Mongols attack Caffa, throwing plague-infested bodies into the city. Plague breaks out in Caffa.

1347   In the fall, the plague travels in ships from Caffa to Sicily, Marseilles, Alexandria, Constantinople, and Spain.

1348   Plague arrives in early winter at Genoa, Pisa, and Venice.

1348	Plague reaches Avignon and Cairo in the spring. Some blame Jews for the the pestilence and attack them.
	Plague surfaces in England and Germany in the summer. The flagellant movement begins.
	Plague comes to London and Ireland in the fall. It reaches Norway in early winter.

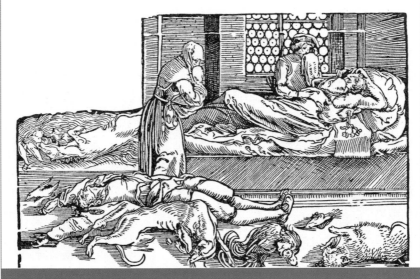

A doctor tends a plague-stricken man surrounded by people and animals killed by the disease in this German illustration from 1532.

1349	Plague reaches Denmark, the Holy Roman Empire, and the Netherlands. The Ordinance of Labourers is passed in England.
1350	Plague arrives in Scotland and Sweden.
1351	Plague strikes Poland and western Russia.

1352	Plague reaches Novgorod, Russia, and comes to an end.
1363	The Sumptuary Laws are passed in England.
1381	The Peasants' Revolt takes place in England.

King Richard II of England and his council sail to meet with rebels in hopes of ending the Peasants' Revolt in 1381.

1453	The Hundred Years' War ends.
1454	Johannes Gutenberg invents the printing press.
1664	The Great Plague of London breaks out.

1666	The Great Fire devastates London, which may have helped to end the outbreak of the plague.

Saint Paul's Cathedral burns during the Great Fire of London.

1771	The last plague epidemic of Europe takes place in Russia.
1894	Alexandre Yersin and Shibasaburo Kitasato identify *Yersinia pestis*.
2007	A fourteen-year-old boy dies of the plague in Mongolia. Authorities contain the outbreak by isolating and treating with antibiotics all people who had had contact with the boy.

GLOSSARY

ANTIBODIES: specialized proteins created by the body to defend it against disease or toxins

ASTROLOGY: the study of the influence of heavenly bodies on human activities

BACTERIUM: a microscopic one-celled organism that is often an agent in infectious disease

BUBO: a lymph node swollen by plague bacteria

BUBONIC PLAGUE: a form of plague transmitted by the bite of a flea, in which bacteria multiply in the lymph nodes

BULL: a formal papal announcement stamped by a bulla, or special seal

CONTAGIOUS: transmittable by direct physical contact

ENZOOTIC: present in a given animal population

EPIDEMIC: a disease outbreak that affects a high percentage of a human population

EPIZOOTIC: a disease outbreak that affects a high percentage of an animal population

FEUDAL: having to do with the social system of the Middle Ages that was based on the relations between lords and their tenants

FLAGELLANTS: a group of Catholics who marched together

and whipped one another to atone for sins thought to have caused the plague

GUILD: an organization of merchants or craftspeople formed for mutual aid and protection

HERESY: religious beliefs or actions that contradict those of the Catholic Church

HUMORS: in ancient and medieval medical theory, the fluids that move through the human body. They include blood, black bile, yellow bile, and phlegm.

IMMUNITY: resistance to infection

INDULGENCES: payment to ensure a reduction of time spent in purgatory before ascending to heaven

INFLUENZA: an acute, contagious illness caused by a virus

LYMPH NODES: areas located in the lymphatic system that filter bacteria and other infectious agents from lymph fluid

MEDIEVAL: having to do with the Middle Ages

PANDEMIC: a disease outbreak that spreads throughout an entire country, continent, or the world

PNEUMONIC PLAGUE: a form of plague that infects the lungs and can spread directly from person to person

POGROM: the organized killing of a group of people, especially Jews

QUARANTINE: isolation, intended to prevent the spread of disease, of those suspected of illness

SACRAMENT: a rite established by the Catholic Church

SEPTICEMIC PLAGUE: a form of plague that infects the bloodstream

TARABAGAN: a marmot, or type of rodent, of the Mongolian steppe

USURY: the practice of lending money and charging interest on the loan

VASSAL: someone who has pledged loyalty to a lord in return for protection

VERNACULAR: the language commonly used in a place

VIRUS: a microscopic agent that reproduces in the cells of living things, causing disease

YEOMEN: in England, a class of landowners below the nobility and above the peasantry

WHO'S WHO?

AVICENNA (ABU ALI AL-HUSAYN IBN ADDALLAH IBN SINA, 980–1037)

Avicenna was born in Bukhara, Iran, and was educated in literature, science, law, and mathematics. He was a renowned physician by the age of sixteen and served as the personal physician to several sultans, or Muslim leaders. He wrote on many subjects. His medical masterpiece, *The Canon of Medicine*, was influential for centuries after his death.

GIOVANNI BOCCACCIO (1313–1375)

Giovanni Boccaccio grew up in Naples and moved to Florence, Italy, in 1341. There he spent his life writing, both scholarly works in Latin and prose and poetry in Italian. His most famous work, *The Decameron*, is set in Florence in 1348, during the plague. His description of the effects of the plague on Florence is renowned. The tales that make up *The Decameron* have influenced writers ever since the work was published.

CHARLES IV, HOLY ROMAN EMPEROR (1316–1378)

Charles IV was born in Prague (in modern Czech Republic) to John of Luxembourg and Elizabeth of Bohemia and raised at the court of King Charles IV of France. He became the ruler of Bohemia and Luxembourg. In 1344 the pope excommunicated the Holy Roman Emperor, Louis, after a long feud, and Louis was deposed in 1346. The pope crowned Charles the Holy Roman Emperor in Rome in

1355. Charles established the first university in central Europe. During the plague years, Charles condemned the pogroms against the Jews in his territories and spoke out against the flagellants. He was relatively powerless to help his people against the plague while it raged.

CLEMENT VI (CA. 1291–1352) Pope Clement VI was born Pierre Roger in France. He was the abbot at two French

monasteries, became archbishop of Sens, and then was made a cardinal. Elected pope in 1342, he was the fourth pope to live in Avignon and refused to return the papacy to Rome. In fact, he bought the city of Avignon from Joanna of Naples. He was known for his extravagant lifestyle and was a patron of artists, writers, and musicians.

EDWARD III (1312–1377) Edward Plantagenet was the son of King Edward II of England. He became king when his father was deposed in 1327 by forces controlled by his father's French wife, Isabella. Much of Edward III's reign was dominated by the Hundred Years' War with France. His constant need for money to fund the war led to increasing power for the Parliament's House of Commons, which was given the right to consent to all forms of taxation.

GALEN OF PERGAMUM (CA. 131–201) Galen was a Greek-born physician and philosopher. He was the physician to the gladiators in Rome and to Emperor Marcus Aurelius. He did experiments and dissections on animals and used his findings about animals' nervous and blood systems as a basis for his work with humans. He developed the theory of the four humors—blood, phlegm, black bile, and yellow bile—that most doctors followed in the Middle Ages. He wrote at least three hundred works on medicine and philosophy, of which half still survive.

GIROLAMO FRACASTORO (1483–1553) Girolamo Fracastoro was born in Verona, Italy. By the age of nineteen, he was a professor of logic and philosophy at the University of Padua. He wrote extensively on the disease syphilis but is best known for his work on communicable diseases, *On Contagion and Contagious Diseases*. In this treatise, he theorized that diseases were spread by living organisms too small to see that were passed from person to person. His theory was not generally accepted for another three centuries.

GUY DE CHAULIAC (CA. 1295–1368) Guy de Chauliac was born in France and educated at the medical school in Montpelier, becoming a master of medicine. Unlike many physicians of the time, he was a practicing surgeon. He became the private physician to Pope Clement VI. He also served the later popes Innocent VI and Urban V. He wrote the surgical text *The Inventory of Medicine*, based on the theories of Galen, which was translated into several languages.

JUSTINIAN (483–565) Justinian was the nephew of Justin I, emperor of the Byzantine Empire. Justininan became emperor in 527 and attempted to assert the supremacy of his rule over that of the church. His greatest accomplishment was the codification of Roman law into the *Corpus juris civilis*. In 541 bubonic plague ravaged his empire. Some historians believe that Justinian himself was stricken but recovered.

SHIBASABURO KITASATO (1852–1931) Shibasaburo Kitasato was a Japanese scientist. Working in Germany, he helped discover the vaccines for diphtheria and tetanus. In 1894 he went to Hong Kong to investigate an outbreak of bubonic plague, and at the same time as Alexandre Yersin, he isolated the plague bacterium, *Yersinia pestis*.

FRANCESCO PETRARCH (1304–1374) Francesco Petrarch was born in Arezzo, Italy, and spent much of his life in Avignon, France. He was a poet, so well-known and popular that he won the honor of being crowned with laurel at Rome for his achievements. He wrote essays and a guidebook to the Holy Land, the lands of the Christian Bible, in Latin and poems in Italian. His poetic style influenced European lyric poets for centuries.

PHILIP VI (1293–1350) King Philip VI of France was the son of Charles of Valois. He was the first French king of the house of Valois, succeeding his cousin, Charles IV. Philip was king during the opening years of the Hundred Years' War with England, losing the important port city of Calais to the English in 1347. The financial losses of the war helped weaken both the French economy and the government.

ALEXANDRE ÉMILE JOHN YERSIN (1863–1943)

Alexandre Yersin was a Swiss bacteriologist and doctor. He worked with Louis Pasteur and helped to develop the antirabies vaccine. He went to Hong Kong in 1894 to investigate an outbreak of pneumonic plague. There, he discovered the bacterium that causes plague. He also found that the bacteria were present in rodent populations.

SOURCE NOTES

4 Johannes de Trokelowe, *Annales*, trans. Brian Tierney, ed. H. T. Riley, Rolls Series, no. 28 (London, 1866), 92–95.

16 Edward III, "Brewers Are Commanded to Use Clean Water," from a document in the Bodleian Library, trans. Stephen Alsford, *Florilegium urbanum—Physical Fabric—Maintaining the Cleanliness of Natural Watercourses*, September 3, 2006, http://www.trytel.com/~tristan/towns/florilegium/community/cmfabr22.html (August 27, 2004).

17 Eileen Edna Power, "The Project Gutenberg EBook of Medieval People," *Medieval People*, n.d., http://www.ibiblio.org/pub/docs/books/gutenberg/1/3/1/4/13144/13144-8.txt (August 9, 2004).

19 Trokelowe, *Annales*, 92–95

20 Frank Stenton, translator, "Ships and Commerce," *Norman London*, Historical Association Leaflet 93, 1934, also available online at http://www.trytel.com/~tristan/towns/florilegium/introduction/intro01.html (August 8, 2008).

22 Procopius, "The Plague, 542 A.D.," *History of the Wars*, book 2, trans. H. B. Dewing, n.d., http://www.gutenberg.org/files/16764/16764-h/16764-h.htm (September 27, 2005).

30 Ibid.

30 Ibid.

34 Rosemary Horrox, ed. and trans., *The Black Death* (Manchester, UK: Manchester University Press, 1994), 17.

36 Agnolo di Tura del Grasso, "The Plague in Siena," *CUA*, n.d., http://faculty.cua.edu/pennington/ChurchHistory220/LectureTen/AgnolodiTura.htm (August 7, 2008).

37 Horrox, *The Black Death*, 36.

38 Ibid.

39 Ibid., 24.

39 Ibid, 36.

40 Giovanni Boccaccio, *The Project Gutenberg Etext of the Decameron*, vol. 1, n.d., http://www.gutenberg.org/dirs/etext03/thdcm10.txt (February 2003).

40 Marchione di Coppo Stefani, "The Florentine Chronicle," *Cronaca fiorentina. Rerum Italicarum Scriptores*, vol. 30, ed. Niccolo Rodolico. Citta di Castello: 1903–1913, translation online at http://www2.iath.virginia.edu/osheim/marchione.html (August 8, 2008).

41 Ibid.

42 di Tura del Grasso, "The Plague in Siena."

44 Horrox, *The Black Death*, 195–197.

45 Stefani, "The Florentine Chronicle."

46 Boccaccio, *The Project Gutenberg Etext of the Decameron.*

46 Stefani, "The Florentine Chronicle."

51 Patricia Willet Cummins, *A Critical Edition of Le Regime Tresutile et Tresproufitable pour Conserver et Garder la Santé du Corps Humain* (Chapel Hill: North Carolina Studies in Romance Languages and Literatures, 1976), also available online at http://www.godecookery.com/regimen/regimen.htm (August 8, 2008).

53 Stefani, "The Florentine Chronicle."

54 Horrox, *The Black Death*, 59.

56 Ibid., 43.

57 Ibid., 159.

58 Ibid., 187.

61 Ibid., 346.

62 Ibid., 122.

63 Ibid., 221.

65 Ibid., 207.

66 Jacob Marcus, *The Jew in the Medieval World: A Sourcebook, 315–1791* (New York: JPS, 1938), 43.

67 Horrox, *The Black Death*, 222.

68 Ibid., 74.

72 Ibid., 250.

73 Ibid., 272.

75 Ibid., 118.

76 Ibid., 82.

82 Ibid., 60.

86 Ibid., 75.

96 Boccaccio, *The Project Gutenberg Etext of the Decameron.*

96 Horrox, *The Black Death*, 248.

96 Francesco Petrarch, "Sonnet 1, On the Announcement of the Death of Laura," *The Project Gutenberg EBook of*

the Sonnets, Triumphs, and
Other Poems of Petrarch, n.d.,
http://www.gutenberg.org/
files/17650/17650-h/17650-h
.htm (January 31, 2006).

98 William Shakespeare,
Romeo and Juliet, n.d.,
http://www.gutenberg.org/
dirs/etext98/2ws1610.txt
(November 1998).

98 Daniel Defoe, A Journal of the
Plague Year, n.d., http://www
.gutenberg.org/files/376/
376-h/766-h.htm (January
16, 2006).

99 Ibid.

102 George Burton Adams and
H. Morse Stephens,, eds.,
Select Documents in English
Constitutional History (New
York: The Macmillan
Company, 1930), also
available online at http://
home.freeuk.net/don-aitken/
ast/e3a.html#69 (August 11,
2008).

104 Ibid.

108 Anna Montgomery
Campbell, The Black Death
and Men of Learning (New
York: Columbia University
Press, 1931), 155.

118 Geoffrey Chaucer, The
Canterbury Tales, n.d.,

http://www.gutenberg.org/
dirs.etext00/ctbls12.txt
(November 2000).

132 Boccaccio, The Project
Gutenberg Etext of the
Decameron.

133 Ibid.

134 Ibid.

135 Ibid.

136 Ibid.

SELECTED BIBLIOGRAPHY

PRIMARY SOURCES

Boccaccio, Giovanni. *The Project Gutenberg Etext of the Decameron*, Vol. 1. N.d. http://www.gutenberg.org/dirs/etext03/thdcm10.txt (February, 2003).

Campbell, Anna Montgomery. *The Black Death and Men of Learning*. New York: Columbia University Press, 1931.

Defoe, Daniel. *A Journal of the Plague Year*. N.d. http://www.gutenberg .org/files/376/376-h/766-h.htm (January 16, 2006).

Di Turo del Grasso, Agnolo. "The Plague in Siena." CUA. N.d. http://faculty.cua.edu/pennington/ChurchHistory220/LectureTen/ AgnolodiTura.html (August 8, 2008).

Horrox, Rosemary, ed. and trans. *The Black Death*. Manchester, UK: Manchester University Press, 1994.

Power, Eileen Edna. "The Project Gutenberg EBook of Medieval People." *Medieval People*. N.d. http://www.ibiblio.org/pub/docs/books/ gutenberg/1/3/1/4/13144/13144-8.txt (August 9, 2004).

Procopius. *History of the Wars*. Book 2. Translated by H. B. Dewing. N.d. http://www.gutenberg.org/files/16764/16764-h/16764-h.htm (September 27, 2005).

Trokelowe, Johannes de. *Annales*, Edited by H. T. Riley. Rolls Series. No. 28. London, 1866.

SECONDARY SOURCES

Benedictow, Ole J. *The Black Death: 1346–1353*. Woodbridge, UK: Boydell Press, 2004.

Bishop, Morris. *The Middle Ages*. New York: American Heritage, 1985.

"The Black Death." *ORB: The Online Reference Book for Medieval Studies*. N.d. http://www.the-orb.net/textbooks/westciv/blackdeath.html (August 7, 2008).

Byrne, Joseph P. *The Black Death*. Westport, CT: Greenwood Press, 2004.

———. *Daily Life during the Black Death*. Westport, CT: Greenwood Press, 2006.

Deaux, George. *The Black Death*. New York: Weybright and Talley, 1969.

Herlihy, David. *The Black Death*. Cambridge, MA: Harvard University Press, 1997.

Jordan, William Chester. *The Great Famine: Northern Europe in the Early Fourteenth Century*. Princeton, NJ: Princeton University Press, 1996.

Kelly, John. *The Great Mortality*. New York: HarperCollins, 2005.

McMullin, Jordan, ed. *Great Disasters: The Black Death*. Farmington Hills, MI: Greenhaven Press, 2003.

Naphy, William, and Andrew Spicer. *The Black Death and the History of Plagues, 1345–1730*. Gloucestershire, UK: Tempus Publishing, 2000.

Nohl, Johannes. *The Black Death*. London: George Allen & Unwin, 1926.

Zebrowski, Ernest, Jr. "The Bubonic Plague." *Fathom: The Source for Online Learning*. N.d. http://www.fathom.com/feature/122201/ (August 7, 2008).

Ziegler, Philip. *The Black Death*. New York: John Day Company, 1969.

FURTHER READING AND WEBSITES

BOOKS

Day, Nancy. *Your Travel Guide to Renaissance Europe*. Minneapolis: Twenty-First Century Books, 2001.

Dunn, John M. *Life during the Black Death*. San Diego: Lucent Books, 2000.

Friedlander, Mark P., Jr. *Outbreak: Disease Detectives at Work*. Minneapolis: Twenty-First Century Books, 2003.

Macdonald, Fiona. *The Plague and Medicine in the Middle Ages*. Milwaukee: World Almanac Library, 2006.

Nardo, Don. *The Black Death*. San Diego: Greenhaven Press, 1999.

Peters, Stephanie True. *The Black Death*. New York: Benchmark Books, 2003.

Senker, Cath. *The Black Death: 1347–1350*. Chicago: Raintree Press, 2006.

Toht, Betony, and Dave Toht. *Daily Life in Ancient and Modern London*. Minneapolis: Lerner Publications, 2001.

WEBSITES

The Black Death. http://history.boisestate.edu/westciv/plague/. Information about the plague and European reactions to it is presented at this site.

CDC Plague Home Page. http://www.cdc.gov/ncidod/dvbid/plague/. This is the Centers for Disease Control and Prevention's page on bubonic plague and its symptoms and transmission.

Community. http://www.trytel.com/~tristan/towns/florilegium/flor02 .html. This site explains how medieval communities were formed and regulated. It includes original source material.

The Decameron Web. http://www.brown.edu/Departments/Italian_Studies/ dweb/plague/index.shtml. This site provides information on the arrival and effects of the plague, as well as some original Italian sources.

Gode Cookery. http://www.godecookery.com/regimen/regimen.htm. A site describing medieval foods, holidays, customs, and medical practices. It includes some primary sources.

Internet Ancient History Sourcebook: Procopius, The Plague. http://www .fordham.edu/halsall/source/542procopius-plague.html. This site provides the ancient historian Procopius's descriptions of the Plague of Justinian.

The Internet Medieval History Sourcebook: The "Calamitous" Fourteenth Century. http://www.fordham.edu/halsall/sbook1w.html#Calamitous %20Century. Read full and partial texts about the plague from medieval sources at this site.

INDEX

ABOUT THE AUTHOR

Diane Zahler studied medieval history in college and has always been fascinated by the bubonic plague. She has written textbooks for students in kindergarten through grade twelve in history, language arts, and literature and is the coauthor of *Test Your Cultural Literacy*, a quiz book, and the author of *The Twenty-First Century Guide to Improving Your Writing*. She lives in Wassaic, New York.

PHOTO ACKNOWLEDGMENTS